W9-BSO-294

Corner to Copa

THE LAST GAME AT
TIGER STADIUM

THE FIRST AT
COMERICA PARK

Illustrations by Mike Thompson, Detroit Free Press editorial cartoonist.

Detroit Free Press

600 W. Fort Street   Detroit, Mich. 48226
www.freep.com

Triumph
BOOKS
CHICAGO

ISBN 1-57243-396-5

Editor: Tom Panzenhagen
Designer: Steve Anderson
Photo editor: Alan R. Kamuda
Photo technician: Rose Ann McKean
Cover design: Steve Dorsey
Comerica Park foldout: Rick Nease
Copy editors: Ken Kraemer, Tim
Marcinkoski
Production editor: Bob Ellis
Special thanks: A.J. Hartley, Dave
Robinson, Christine Russell, Shelly
Solon and the Free Press sports staff.

Other recent books by the Free Press sports staff:
State of Glory   Century of Champions
The Corner   Believe!
M1CH1GAN   Stanleytown
To order, call 800-245-5082 or go to www.freep.com/bookstore

Cover: Comerica Park inaugural, April 11,
2000 by Mary Schroeder/Detroit Free Press

ROOM WITH A VIEW

By Mitch Albom

ERIC SEALS

GABRIEL B. TAIT

Opening Day 2000: With downtown as a backdrop, fans swarmed the streets around Detroit's new marquee attraction — Comerica Park.

W e would not see snow. We would not see cold. We ignored the icy water as we sloshed through city streets.

"Wind? What w-w-wind?" we said, as we marched to the gates. "We don't feel any w-w-wind."

Those were not parkas wrapped around our bodies. Those were not gloves or boots or scarves.

"Ski cap?" we said, as we

moved through the turnstiles. "What ski cap? Oh, *that* thing?"

We refused to see winter. We refused to see gray. On this first day of baseball in the first year of the new century, in April weather better suited to January, the people of Detroit had eyes for one thing and one thing only.

The New House.

It is spectacular.

At 1:18 Tuesday afternoon, April 11, 2000, the first pitch was thrown in Comerica Park, our first new baseball stadium in 88 years, and for a blessed moment the cold seemed to halt and the sun seemed to rise, and we opened our eyes to a single most impressive thing. It was not the pristine field, the massive scoreboard, the carousel, the Ferris wheel, the fountains with fireworks or the food spots with everything from elephant ears to beef brisket.

No. The most impressive thing inside this new stadium was the view out. For when you look to the outfield, you see buildings, windows, rooftops, chimneys. You see the Cadillac Tower, the Detroit Opera House, the Renaissance Center, the blinking red ball atop the Penobscot Building. You see offices, hotels, corporate headquarters, standing like sentinels, peeking onto the field. It's as if this massive structure were dropped smack into the middle of a metropolis. A tree grows in Brooklyn?

A ballpark grows in Detroit.

"This is awesome," said Lance Parrish, the Tigers' star catcher >>

J. KYLE KEENER

Before the first game, grounds keeper Matt McQuaid made sure Comerica Park was free of snowbanks.

turned Tigers coach, as he gazed around the upper decks and the exposed steel beams and trusses, painted dark green, resembling something out of a Paris train station. "Everything you want, you got here."

Everything you want. Anything you can think of. Wasn't this the most common pose at the opener: people walking, dazed, mouths open, looking left, right, up, down, like country folk let into the royal castle? A sea of fans clogged in the new concourses, barely noticing that they weren't moving because look, there's Ty Cobb, look, there's a gourmet pretzel place, look, there's a carousel, look, there's a bat-shaped tower of Tigers history, one for the 1920s, one for the 1940s, one for the 1960s, '70s, '80s.

And then, the most impressive part, as fans came out into the light, the wide-open spaces, and their eyes traveled across the grassy outfield, over the large bullpen, over the orange umbrellas of the picnic porch above rightfield, and up, up, up into that skyline view, looking as if they had never seen the city before. And perhaps some of them hadn't. But they were seeing it now.

A curtain lifts.

A ballpark grows in Detroit.

"We got it finished," a relieved John McHale, the Tigers' president, said just before the opening ceremonies. "There are still some cords here and there, some construction here or there. But we're ready for baseball."

He laughed.

"And I don't think you have to worry about stepping on a loose board and disappearing."

Not that anyone would have noticed. The overwhelming reaction from the 39,168 capacity crowd was positive, welcoming, impressed, awestruck, even giddy at the idea that we get to use this place not one day or one season but for years to come.

And here, in the year 2000, only the most traditional or cynical will complain. It feels right. It feels like progress. Sure, there is a tug of history down the street, at Michigan and Trumbull, where old Tiger Stadium stands alone as a Roman ruin. But the new ballpark celebrates history, too. There are the aforementioned bat towers of decades past and the impressive statues in left-centerfield of Ty Cobb, Hank Greenberg, Charlie Gehringer, Hal Newhouser, Al Kaline.

There was, before the first pitch, the passing of the Tigers' team flag that flew at Tiger Stadium and now flies at Comerica, hoisted on a left-centerfield flagpole, still the only one in baseball that is in the field of play.

And when they started the game, it sure looked like the old baseball. There was a called strike for the first pitch, there were two triples — proving the far-out fences may engender fewer home runs and more baserunning — and there was even a stellar defensive play, when first baseman Tony Clark dove for a sinking liner, caught it, popped up and then dove again for a tag on the retreating runner — got him — an unassisted double play.

And, oh yes, the Tigers won, 5-2, over the Seattle Mariners, christening the place with baseball's sweetest moisture, the sweat of victory.

Were there problems? There are always problems. Parking was a headache, traffic didn't flow well, lines were long at concession stands.

But you can fix those things. What you can't fix, what you couldn't create, were little things that never existed at Tiger Stadium. Like limousines pulling up to the different entrances, entrances you could see from inside the building as you walked around, giving the place a Hollywood opening night feel. Like people gathered outside the stadium outfield, peeking in through the fences, watching the game, people you could see from inside as well.

Like people standing out near the fountains that explode after home runs — running for cover when the wind blew the water streams down on them like rain. ➤➤

JUNE 18, 1998

APRIL 12, 1999

MARCH 29, 2000

KENT PHILLIPS

**Fans clambered for a peek inside the field of dreams,
where concourses were a swirl of activity.**

DAVID P. GILKEY

Can you imagine that in summer? Kids will have their shirts off, hoping for a splash from the city's biggest sprinkler system.

In fact, you can imagine families coming downtown and visiting the stadium even *without* tickets, taking photos in front of those statues of Tigers legends, checking out the Ferris wheel, sneak-peeking a few innings through the metal gates. You can hear them saying, "Let's go to the city and hang around near the stadium."

A ballpark grows in Detroit.

I have never been a person who says stadiums save cities. They don't. They never have. But Opening Day 2000 was an instructive day for us. For just as we denied the winter freeze, just as we saw through the gray and the cold because we wanted to — so, too, are we capable of seeing past the

ugly part of this city's history, past the decay, past the prejudices and misconceptions that suggest Detroit can never come back.

Why not? Why St. Louis and not here? Why Cleveland and not here? We have a gem at the new corner, Montcalm and Brush, a sports cathedral to be proud of, a site to take visiting family and friends to, and, more important, a site they will *ask* to visit.

And when they look out over the field, they — and maybe you — will see something that has always been there, but for some reason was nearly invisible. They will see buildings, lights, people, traffic.

They will see a city.

A ballpark grows in Detroit. And here is the best part. You think it's nice now?

Just wait till it stops snowing. ◆

SEPTEMBER 27, 1999

GRAND FINALE

By Bill McGraw

ERIC SEALS

The Corner rocked. Music blared. Flashbulbs popped. Strangers talked baseball to strangers. On the final day at Tiger Stadium, fans were treated to a festive wake that featured heavy nostalgia, 63 old-time players, and a rooftop grand slam. The daylong celebration concluded with an emotional ceremony in which groundskeeper Charlie McGee dug up home plate with a pickax and took the precious cargo in a motorcade across downtown to the new Comerica Park.

Moments later, a cast of former Tigers took their former positions to loud applause and participated in a ceremonial lowering of the stadium flag.

The evening ended with many of the 43,356 fans standing at their seats, piano music playing over the public-address system, and the lights slowly going dark.

As some fans dabbed tears from their eyes and others beamed wide smiles, beloved announcer Ernie Harwell bid farewell to one of the most historic pieces of baseball real estate in America.

"Tonight, we say good-bye," Harwell said. "Farewell, old friend Tiger Stadium. We will remember."

As fans trooped down the stadium ramps for the final time, Darren Butti of Warren stopped just outside the leftfield stands. Turning to his wife and a friend, he said: "All right, I'm going to take one last look. Then I'm going to go home and cry."

Detroit Mayor Dennis Archer said: "It was almost like being in baseball church."

In whatever way one measured the stadium's longevity — as a 103-year-old site for pro baseball or as an 87-year-old stadium — the final game was one for the ages, young

Pete Simakas of Dearborn Heights had a date with destiny.

J. KYLE KEENER

and old. It was the 6,873rd major league game at The Corner since 1912, and it had something for everyone. The home team even won, 8-2.

Caressed by a warm autumn sun, fans began arriving at Michigan and Trumbull hours before the 4:09 p.m. first pitch. Radio stations hosted parties behind several nearby bars and, by noon, hard-driving rock tunes serenaded the gleeful throngs that were spilling onto sidewalks. Inside the park, the muggy old corridors were gridlocked throughout the game as fans jockeyed for their final beers, hot dogs and $10 programs.

Despite the crowds around the park, the day came off peacefully. Police arrested only nine persons for disorderly conduct, at least four

of whom had jumped onto the field. One man was arrested on a larceny charge for allegedly trying to steal an armrest from a stadium seat, said Detroit police chief Benny Napoleon, who headed an immense police presence.

"We didn't anticipate there would be any problems, but we were prepared in case anyone had the inclination," Napoleon said.

As fans entered the stadium, Tigers staffers embossed their tickets with a special final-day stamp, and fans protected their prized tickets in plastic ID tags hanging around their necks, as though they had been issued special credentials for the day.

Seeing the game was hardly important to some fans. Being there was all that mattered.

"Just to get any seat is OK," said Bert Ferraro of Buffalo, N.Y. He paid $450 for eight seats in the lower leftfield deck that normally sold for $6.25 each. Worse, though, was that Ferraro couldn't see the game. He was sitting directly behind a steel pillar marked "Sec. 502." Obstructed view. But his wife, Claudia, didn't care. "This is Tiger Stadium!" she said. "There's so much history here, just to be ➤➤

KIRTHMON F. DOZIER

Scores of fans waited for gates to open and turnstiles to tumble one last time, while tiger lady Angel Cauchon curbed her emotions beneath a Michigan Avenue lamppost.

J. KYLE KEENER

CORNER TO COPA

inside is so unbelievable!"

And there were celebrities galore.

Junk-bond king and financier Michael Milken quietly entered the ballpark, noting his first visit was in 1974. "I was a huge Hank Greenberg fan," Milken said. He also was partial to Al Kaline, another Hall of Famer.

Milken was in a giving mood. A prostate cancer survivor, he offered to donate $50,000 to prostate cancer research for every home run hit during the finale. The gesture cost him $200,000.

Edsel Ford, a longtime fan who already had tickets to Comerica Park, said the closing-day crowd was astonishing, even compared to the 1984 World Series. "I don't ever remember seeing a crowd like this," he said.

Gordie Howe, a genius on skates, walked into the stadium past Ty Cobb's bronze plaque that lionizes the "genius in spikes." Howe said: "Coming here today is something every kid wants to do."

Paul Siden of Huntington Woods stood next to the Cobb plaque, wearing an antique baseball glove. Siden, who paid $60 for a $5 bleacher seat, said, "I've been to a million games here. I just had to go to the last one."

Friendliness abounded. Fans >>

NOTICE
FOR THE COMFORT & SAFETY OF ALL FANS

FINAL GAME TICKETS
WILL BE EMBOSSED AS
FANS ENTER THE STADIUM

↑ PROGRAMS ↑

TIGER STADIUM

Baseball has been played on this site since before 1900 and it has been the home of the Detroit Tigers from their start as a charter member of the American League in 1901.

TYRUS RAYMOND COBB
1886 — 1961

GREATEST TIGER OF ALL
A GENIUS IN SPIKES

Faces in the crowd included Tigers players, who greeted many fortunate fans. Dan Balice and son John, from Ionia, were among those who paused for pictures in front of The Corner's commemorative plaques. And Ty was there, too — Ty Currie of Grand Blanc — perched atop his dad's shoulders, calling for a program.

 13

KIRTHMON F. DOZIER (4)

Closing-day Tigers honored their all-time teammates, among them: Dean Palmer donned George Kell's No. 21, Dave Mlicki borrowed Mickey Lolich's No. 29, Jeff Weaver wore Hal Newhouser's No. 14 and Karim Garcia was all right in Al Kaline's No. 6.

In the end, the grass was green, the hot dogs hot and stadium worker Courtney Porter letter-perfect.

Can I have your autograph? Gabe Kapler obliged Kelly Brown of Dearborn Heights and Melissa Duran of Lincoln Park, while Clair Kuhn of Madison Heights, below, waited anxiously. Meanwhile, Dave Mlicki (with camera) and C.J. Nitkowski didn't miss a pitch.

Getting the scoop on the finale were 6-year-old Max Acheson of West Bloomfield and Rob Andreozzi of Warren.

reminisced with strangers. Detroit police officers obliged visitors by taking their photographs. Many current Tigers took photos.

Brett Endelman of Bloomfield Hills showed up in a Santa Claus suit, warm day and all. Mike Heiwig and Frank Pollina, both of Birmingham, came adorned in tuxedos with orange boutonnieres, a Tigers touch. "Next to my wedding, there is no other event I can think of that warrants me wearing a tuxedo like the last game at Tiger Stadium," Pollina said.

William Green always had wanted to visit Tiger Stadium. Only 6, he got a doozy to remember. The Adrian youngster attended the historic game as a birthday present and got to skip first grade for a day. He figured his teacher would understand. "You learn more about sports here," the veteran T-ball player said, his expression a model of seriousness.

Playing hooky with Green was 9-year-old Derek Rymill of Sterling Heights, whose father surprised him with tickets. "I just wish they wouldn't tear this thing down," Derek lamented.

Even Tigers outfielder Kimera Bartee dug what was going on.

Game programs were hot — and scarce. Tracking down a program was a tough quest. John Morgan of Warren said he tried for more than 30 minutes to get his hands on one. "It's terrible," he said. A vendor "said he'd be back in 10 — he never came back."

Bub Mueray stood on Michigan Avenue, camera in hand, looking for any gap he could find in a large white canvas tarp that was hanging inside the fence of the Tiger Plaza

picnic area. On the other side was a pregame gathering of former Tigers stars, and Mueray succeeded.

"This is awesome," he said, noting he had clicked off a few frames of players. "It's nice to see the old, old players come back. It's like a reunion."

Others had their own reunions. At Sportsland USA outside the park, customers streamed in to say good-bye to store owner Neil Heffernan, including the first customer he had when the store opened 25 years ago. Despite brisk sales of hats and T-shirts, Heffernan was melancholy. "It's a bittersweet day, but mostly bitter," he said.

The sentiment was echoed by others who relied on the stadium for their living. Irene Sember, 77, had been parking cars at a lot adjacent to her home for 29 seasons. Customers from as far away as Grand Rapids and Kalamazoo brought her cards, flowers and a thank-you scrapbook as they drove in for the final time.

"I sure know a lot of people," she said. "I don't have to get out there to wave a flag. They come right to me." Sember said she didn't know what she would do without the income she got from parking cars. Some lot owners raised prices for the final game, but Sember remained true to her season-long $10 tariff. "A beautiful lady with integrity and a survival instinct," Juli Clark of Ferndale wrote in Sember's scrapbook. "After parking at Irene's, nowhere else would do."

Rob Wagner of Trenton bent over a waist-high railing and scooped up dirt. He plans to keep it at home, where some sod from the 1984 World Series finale grows in his backyard. "I grew up here," said Wagner, a former stadium employee who shagged foul balls from a stool near the bullpen.

For one day, old favorites such as Jack Morris, Dave Rozema and Kirk Gibson walked the main corridor with mere mortals such as attorney Joseph Sullivan, who summed up the joyous mood: "They should close this stadium every day." One fan described himself as angry. He was Frank Rashid, a founder of the Tiger Stadium fan club that tried to save the park.

"There is not one economist in the country who would agree that closing this stadium and moving to Comerica is smart public policy," said Rashid, who sat in rightfield.

The game highlight was Robert Fick's bases-loaded home run that slammed onto the roof in rightfield and bounced back into the outfield.

The blast iced the game for the Tigers, and Fick, hardly a household name, signed autographs well into the night.

Another homer came off the bat of Tigers rightfielder Karim Garcia. In the upper-leftfield seats, James Minella of Clinton Township cradled the ball as if it were a newborn. Minella has the distinction of being the last fan to catch a homer in the old stadium. "If it is the last home run caught and it's a piece of history, it's pretty cool," Minella said.

After the game, fans grew hoarse cheering for the former Tigers who entered the field from centerfield for the closing ceremony as music from the film "Braveheart" played. First to appear was Mark (The Bird) Fidrych, the sensation of the mid-1970s who ran to the pitcher's mound and scooped dirt into a plastic bag.

Players who received some of the loudest cheers were hometown favorites Willie Horton, Gibson and Ron LeFlore. Fans also screamed for Alan Trammell, Lou Whitaker, Gates Brown and Al Kaline. Some fans seemed stunned to see such long-forgotten heroes as Jim Bunning, Eddie Yost and Charlie (Paw Paw) Maxwell.

"Awesome, just awesome," gushed Richard Coriaty, a former Detroiter who traveled from Fontana, Calif., for the game. Coriaty swept his hand toward the field, where the players assembled, dressed in the plain white uniforms with the Olde English D on their chest. "You know, of all the things that have happened in this city, the one thing we all have in common is those guys out there," he said.

And the old building that became our field of dreams. ◆

CARLOS OSORIO / Associated Press

Players and fans stood for the national anthem one last time.

THE SPIRIT OF THE TIGERS

Dressed in full uniform, crisp and white in the sun, Al Kaline stood silently, allowing the applause to wash over him. He looked down. He shuffled his feet. He paced in front of the pitcher's mound, nervous, trying to keep from weeping.

Before the final game of Tiger Stadium's life, Kaline delivered the eulogy.

At 64, the Hall of Famer looked a little like a kid again. Felt like it, too. He recalled the first time he saw the park, in 1953, when he was an 18-year-old rookie fresh off the train from his hometown of Baltimore.

From the outside, it "looked like an impressive battleship, a fortress at Michigan and Trumbull," he said. From the inside, it held a brilliant patch of emerald-green grass, faint smells of beer and sausages, and a "peacefulness that seemed almost magical."

"Yes," Kaline said, "on that day, I was awestruck…. Yet today, 46 years later, I stand before you as a grown man, a veteran of thousands of games in this ballpark, and again find myself humbled and somewhat overwhelmed by the events unfolding in front of us…. There is just too much history here to summarize that effectively."

The weight of the moment was not lost. As fans, officials and former players counted down the

JULIAN H. GONZALEZ

Al Kaline, who provided countless memories during 22 seasons in a Tigers uniform, added a few more with a stirring farewell address.

hours and minutes to game time, each summoned memories. Even summer itself seemed to stop by for the final game, with the afternoon air at 84 degrees.

About noon, Tigers alumni from as early as the 1930s began gathering in Tiger Plaza for a reception, as fans peeked through the iron gates to catch a glimpse. Everyone wanted to crash the party, including Red Wings great Gordie Howe, who somehow got in without a pass.

Jim Northrup, a member of the 1968 champions, sat in the shade

with a soft drink. He recalled 1975, when he was with Baltimore. He knew he was about to retire, so the last time the Orioles visited Tiger Stadium, he arrived early and sat in the dugout for two hours, just looking around.

Darrell Evans, a member of the 1984 champions, leaned against a wall, speaking softly. He woke up early, came downtown with his family about 9:30 a.m., and took a tour of local bars and restaurants. When he finally approached the stadium, he looked at the crowd outside and felt a loss.

"This was the best place ever to play baseball," he said. "Just the smell. Just the atmosphere. The people were right on top of you. They were part of you. I can see them in my mind all the time. I didn't want this to be a sad day, but I guess it is.

"I wish I'd spent my whole career here," Evans said. "I really do."

About 45 minutes before the game, the ceremony began. Owner Mike Ilitch, Mayor Dennis Archer, Gov. John Engler and baseball commissioner Bud Selig spoke — the higher the office, the louder the boos. But upon being introduced by legendary broadcaster Ernie Harwell — who received a 40-second standing ovation — Kaline kept them standing and screaming for 76 seconds.

"If any player defined the spirit of the Tigers in the second half of the century," Harwell said, "it was No. 6."

The crowd roared. With shadows starting to creep across the field, Kaline approached the microphone. The initials "J. C." and "N. C." were written on his cap in memory of late friends — former general manager Jim Campbell and former teammate Norm Cash.

Kaline gulped. Then he summed it all up.

"We are truly fortunate that Tiger Stadium has been a place that rises above the success of the home team," he said. "The Tiger Stadium experience is about so much more than just winning and losing. It is a bond that nearly all the people of Detroit share… .

"Tiger Stadium's strengths lie not in its dazzling architecture or creature comforts, but rather in its character, charm and history. And while common materials may have been used to build this place … the memories are the cement that has held it together for 88 wonderful seasons." ◆
– By Nicholas J. Cotsonika

KALINE'S ADDRESS

Thank you very much. What a great day.

I have often spoken of the first time I entered Tiger Stadium as an 18-year-old back in 1953. From the outside, coming from the old train station just down the street, how the ballpark looked like an impressive battleship, a fortress at Michigan and Trumbull.

But then inside, coming through the aisles and seeing the field, the green, green grass and the thousands of seats around, and even more the peacefulness that seemed almost magical.

Yes, on that day, I was awestruck. As a kid fresh out of high school, I suppose that was only natural.

Yet today, 46 years later, I stand before you as a grown man, a veteran of thousands of games in this ballpark, and again find myself humbled and somewhat overwhelmed by the events unfolding in front of us.

Today I have been asked to speak for the more than 1,300 players who have had the great fortune to wear the Olde English D. My goal, my responsibility, should be to put into words what this ballpark has meant to each of us.

But I do not pretend to understand the role that Tiger Stadium, Briggs Stadium, Navin Field has played in the lives and the careers of my colleagues. There is just too much history here to summarize that effectively.

We are truly fortunate that Tiger Stadium has been a place that rises above the success of the home team. The Tiger Stadium experience is about so much more than just winning and losing. It is a bond that nearly all the people of Detroit share.

Looking back on the last century, so many events have played a critical role in Detroit's past are associated in some way with Tiger Stadium. More often than not, that has proved a respite during hard times, whether it was a diversion for those in despair during the Depression, or the healing effect during the difficult, turbulent times in the late '60s.

And during the good times, it was a gathering place for celebration, a shared experience for people from all walks of life.

The ballpark has grown hand-in-hand with the city. Tiger Stadium's strengths lie not in its dazzling architecture or creature comforts, but rather in its character, charm and history.

And while common materials may have been used to build this place — concrete, steel and bricks — the memories are the cement that has held it together for 88 wonderful seasons.

Though we are saddened and nostalgic on this occasion, the time is right to move on. With a wonderful new ballpark rising just a mile away, we look forward to a promising future that will be filled by the memories of our old home.

I summarize and conclude my thoughts today with a question to be answered by each of you. Is it a specific game that you will remember most about Tiger Stadium? Maybe Ty Cobb sliding hard into third, George Kell diving to his left, Norm Cash or Kirk Gibson blasting one into the lights in rightfield?

Or will it be a memory of your family and friends, sharing a story with your best buddy, or listening closely as your dad tells you of the first time he came to the ballpark years ago?

For me, for most, I trust the answer involves a little bit of both.

Thank you. ◆

CARLOS OSORIO / Associated Press

Hall of Famers George Brett of Kansas City and Detroit's Al Kaline exchanged lineup cards and more.

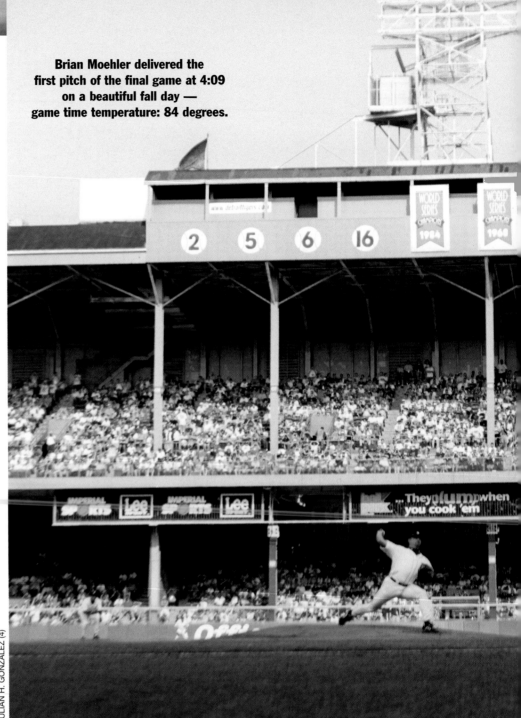

Brian Moehler delivered the
first pitch of the final game at 4:09
on a beautiful fall day —
game time temperature: 84 degrees.

JULIAN H. GONZALEZ (4)

TIGERS 8, ROYALS 2

THE LONG GOOD-BYE

By John Lowe

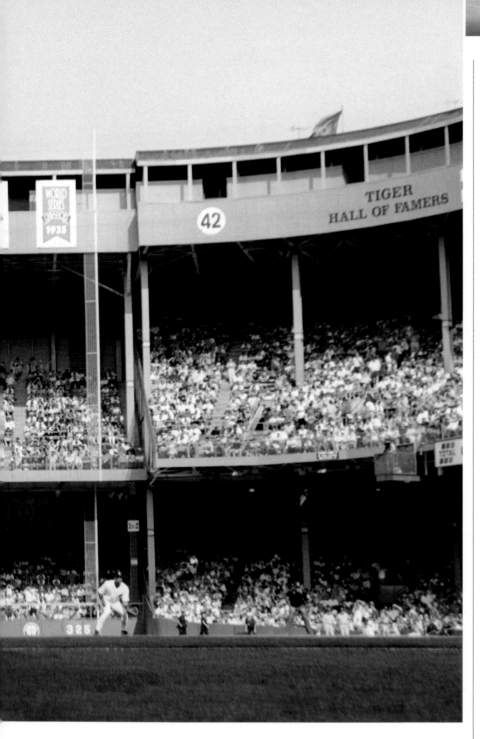

But it didn't quite make it.

No matter. Fick's NASA shot off Jeff Montgomery clinched the Tigers' 8-2 victory. The fans roared in jubilation worthy of a World Series as Fick slowly circled the bases. It was reminiscent of another eighth-inning, close-out homer: Kirk Gibson's second-deck blast off San Diego's Goose Gossage — to the same part of the park — in Game 5 of the 1984 World Series that clinched the Tigers' title.

Fick's roof shot was the final hit at Tiger Stadium.

Right-hander Todd Jones retired Kansas City in order in the ninth, ending it by getting Carlos Beltran swinging on a 2-2 slow curve at 7:07 p.m. on the scoreboard clock. The pitch broke inside and landed near the plate. Catcher Brad Aumsus stopped the ball on a hop and tagged Beltran, who made no attempt to run from the left-handed batter's box.

Beltran turned out to be the American League rookie of the year. But the day belonged to The Corner, the 104-year veteran. And the final pitch ever at Michigan and Trumbull was the most photographed ever.

So many hundreds of cameras flashed during Beltran's at-bat that plate umpire Rocky Roe said, "It was like looking into the Milky Way."

The Tigers won the last three Tiger Stadium games from the Royals, matching their longest winning streak of the dismal 1999 season, and the victory carried special significance. Club president John McHale asked players before the game to win, however they did it. Jones called it the biggest game of the Tigers' season. Ausmus said there was an urgency to win.

Yet with a few hits in the right places, it could have been Kansas City romping to victory. The Royals created more strong threats than the Tigers, but they hit only ➤➤

T iger Stadium will be remembered above all for power hitting. That's true whether you saw hundreds of games there — or only the finale.

Luis Polonia, a 5-foot-8 outfielder, led off the Tigers' first inning with a monstrous homer to right-center. Then, with the score tied in the sixth, Karim Garcia lofted an opposite-field drive a few rows into the upper deck in left,

putting the Tigers in front for good.

And then — oh, my! — with one out in the eighth, rookie Robert Fick rocketed a grand slam off the rightfield roof — straight toward Comerica Park. The ball hit just to the foul-pole side of the light standard nearest the pole. For a second or two, everyone waited to see if it would bounce over the roof and become the final roof-clearing homer at Tiger Stadium.

one homer, Mark Quinn's solo shot. In the key stat of the day, the Royals' fourth, fifth and sixth hitters were 2-for-10 with runners in scoring position.

Tigers starter Brian Moehler gave up nine hits and two walks in six innings, and manager Larry Parrish said he was close to coming out of the game for Nelson Cruz in the third and fifth innings. "Moehler had nothing," Parrish said.

But the right-hander, to whom Parrish gave the closing-day assignment because he was the team's senior starting pitcher, won the game by doing what a veteran starter is supposed to do: He did his best pitching with the other team threatening. He held those 4-5-6 hitters to one hit in seven at-bats with runners in scoring position.

In raising his record to 10-16, Moehler qualified for the same compliment that Dodgers announcer Vin Scully gave Fernando Valenzuela after a 5-4 win in the World Series: "It wasn't Fernando's best game, just his greatest."

Joe Randa's day summed up how an 8-2 game is a game of inches (or "fractions of inches," as an old-timer once said). The near misses for the former Tiger began with two out in the first and the bases loaded. Moehler got a pitch up, and Randa whistled a line drive toward right-center. The smash could have given Kansas City a 2-0 or 3-0 lead. But second baseman Damion Easley didn't need to move to catch it. And the day's first run came moments later, when Polonia launched Jeff Suppan's 1-2 pitch an estimated 435 feet, into the far section of the lower deck in right-center.

Randa (who went from the Tigers to the Mets to the Royals before the 1999 season) singled in a run in the third, tying it at 2. But the hit didn't have nearly the ➤➤

JULIAN H. GONZALEZ

"I was just trying to make contact with two strikes," Luis Polonia said.
He did, connecting for a leadoff homer that brought teammates to their feet.

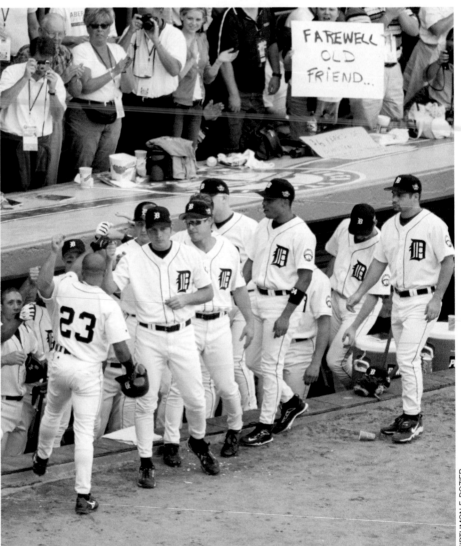

KIRTHMON F. DOZIER

GOOD OL' NO. 6

Outfielder Karim Garcia said he hoped he could live up to the honor of wearing Al Kaline's No. 6 in the finale. And then Garcia proceeded to have a Kaline-type game, making all the plays in rightfield, hitting the cutoff man regularly, uncorking a crisp throw home that arrived on target on the fly to hold a runner at third, and then capping the all-around performance with a tie-breaking, two-run homer in the bottom of the sixth that turned out to be the winning hit.

After the game, someone asked Garcia if he thought he could talk the Tigers into giving him No. 6 permanently. "I wish," Garcia said, laughing, "but I don't think that's going to happen. I'm just happy I was able to do some good things while I was wearing his number. I put my team ahead with a home run, made a couple of nice plays in the outfield — it made me feel good."

Karim Garcia had Kansas City's number — his two-run homer in the sixth put the Tigers ahead, 4-2, and earned him a high-five.

Garcia wasn't the only Tiger who gained inspiration from wearing the uniform number of Tigers greats who preceded them.

■ Starter **Brian Moehler** — wearing No. 47 and doing his best Jack Morris imitation — got out of a bases-loaded jam in the first inning when it looked as if the Royals were about to do some real damage. Moehler was credited with a blue-collar type victory, just the kind that Morris would have been proud of.

■ **Robert Fick** — wearing Norm Cash's No. 25 — delivered a sacrifice fly with one out and a runner on third in the second inning, then put the icing on the cake with a monstrous eighth-inning grand slam that bounced off the rightfield roof.

■ **Doug Brocail** — wearing John Hiller's No. 18 — came in with the bases loaded and one out in the seventh inning and threw a double-play ball to protect a two-run lead.

Footnote: Players didn't wear numbers in the early part of the 20th Century, so centerfielder Gabe Kapler didn't wear one either, in honor of Ty Cobb's presence on the all-time Tigers team. ◆

– *By Gene Guidi*

JULIAN H. GONZALEZ (2)

JULIAN H. GONZALEZ

impact it could have because Mike Sweeney — the previous hitter — had hit into a double play on a cut fastball after the first two hitters of the inning singled. Sweeney also swung at and missed a cut fastball for strike three with one out and the bases loaded in the first.

In the fifth, Beltran nearly homered to put Kansas City ahead. His leadoff drive on a change-up — his third straight hit on Moehler's off-speed pitch — hit the fence in center. Moehler kept it tied by retiring those 4-5-6 hitters: Jermaine Dye on a fly ball, Sweeney on a called third strike on the outer edge of the plate ("a pitcher's pitch," Ausmus said), then Randa on a grounder to third.

An inning later, the Inches Game caught up with Randa on defense. Tigers third baseman Dean Palmer — whose free-agent departure from Kansas City opened a spot for Randa — led off the Tigers' sixth with a hard grounder to Randa's left. The third baseman dove for it, but it rolled off his glove toward short for an infield single.

Easley bunted Palmer to second, only his second sacrifice of the season. Garcia conked Suppan's 1-1

They didn't have front-row seats, like some, but former Tigers Gates Brown (seated) and Tom Brookens were on hand for the finale.

GABRIEL B. TAIT

pitch the other way, upstairs. Garcia has made a habit of delivering homers in close games — it was his 13th of the season, and his 11th with the difference in the game three runs or fewer. (The Tigers' closing power show illustrated the park's variety: of their three homers, one landed in the lower deck, one

in the upper deck and one on the roof.)

After Garcia's homer made it 4-2, rookie Francisco Cordero relieved Moehler to start the seventh, and the first two hitters reached base — bringing up those 4-5-6 hitters one more time.

Cordero whiffed Dye. Sweeney — who had fanned twice and hit into the crucial double play — batted with a runner in scoring position for the fourth time in as many at-bats. He singled sharply to right, but Rey Sanchez held at third, filling the bases.

Doug Brocail relieved to face Randa, taking his fourth at-bat with a runner in scoring position. A single would have tied the game. Randa grounded into a double play that first baseman Tony Clark completed with an excellent pickup of shortstop Deivi Cruz's throw.

Again, the mood of the party had been saved.

Then Fick came up in the eighth.

In "The Maltese Falcon," Casper Gutman tells Sam Spade, "The shortest farewells are the best."

Not always.

Fick walloped The Long Goodbye, and it was glorious. ◆

CORNER TO COPA

GABRIEL B. TAIT

As usual, longtime Tigers broadcaster Ernie Harwell had the best seat in the house.

J. KYLE KEENER (2)

Fans roared their approval throughout the game. Grounds crew member Wesley Easley even put on a show between innings.

> **" I looked up in the sky
> and thought of my dad. "**
> – Robert Fick

SLAM BAM

Before Robert Fick was due to bat in the bottom of the eighth inning, manager Larry Parrish pulled him aside and said: "I think I'm going to pinch-hit Frank (Catalanotto) for you."

Fick met his manager's gaze and replied: "I'm not going to smile about this if that's what you're waiting for." Fick convinced Parrish that he was the right hitter to face Kansas City right-hander Jeff Montgomery, so the manager changed his mind about replacing the designated hitter.

It might have been the best decision the manager made all year.

With the bases loaded and one out, Fick blasted what would be the last home run at Tiger Stadium, a majestic drive that kept climbing and climbing, finally hitting the roof above the third deck in right-field before bouncing back onto the field.

As he rounded the bases, Fick looked up and mouthed a silent greeting to his father, Charles, who died in November 1998 of congestive heart failure at 69.

"I looked up in the sky and thought of my dad," Fick said. "I felt that he was up there watching me, that he was with me as I went around the bases. I'm dedicating the home run to him. I just know

he had something to do with all of this. I was always the little guy that he said could do big things."

Fick, 25, grew up a Tigers fan in Sparky Anderson's hometown of Thousand Oaks, Calif. Fick's first impression of Tiger Stadium was, "It's a little ballpark, but it's so high. I've never seen anything like it.

"To be able to say I was on the last team to ever play at Tiger Stadium is probably something I'd wished for as a little kid.

"This is definitely the most exciting thing that's ever happened to me," Fick said of his grand slam. "It was just an unbelievable feeling to do something like that for the team and for all the people who came out to say good-bye to this park." ◆
– *By Gene Guidi*

JULIAN H. GONZALEZ (2)

The crowning moment came in the bottom of the eighth as Robert Fick raised the roof with a grand slam. The final runners to cross home plate were, from left: Damion Easley, Fick, Gabe Kapler and Karim Garcia.

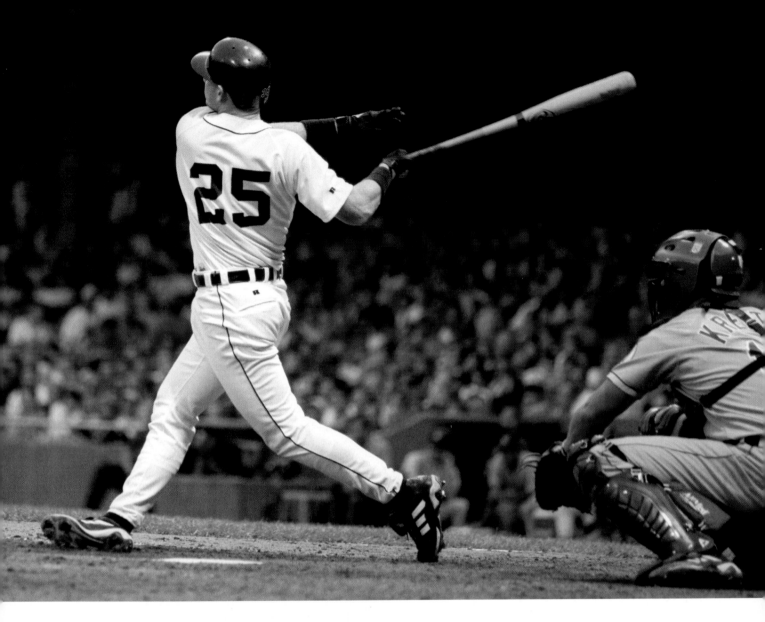

GR-R-REAT!

Maybe Robert Fick's grand slam in the grand finale will become more than a vivid moment in Tigers history. Maybe it will inspire the rest of Fick's career.

Kirk Gibson talked to him about it afterward.

"I told him there are times in this game when you might doubt yourself, and you might be struggling a little bit, and you're going to come up in a real pressure situation," Gibson said. "You've got to have affirmation that you love pressure situations and that you perform even better in them.

"You have to have something you can visualize so you can print that thought in your mind. When you do print it in your mind, that's a very powerful moment, because sometimes you don't believe in yourself in this game.

"Now he's got something, and he'll never forget it. A packed house. Anticipation. Bases are juiced. Last game at Tiger Stadium. He'll never forget the feeling when the ball went off his bat."

Someone else who might never forget is Kansas City Royals right-hander Jeff Montgomery, who served up the slam. Here's what he was thinking when Fick batted with the bases loaded and one out in the eighth inning:

"I had never faced him. I was hopeful of throwing a fastball down and away and getting a ground ball up the middle for a double play. The ball leaped to the middle-inside part of the plate. For most left-handed hitters, that's a fairly hot zone. He jumped on it. That was it."

Fick produced Tiger Stadium's final roof shot, final homer, final runs and hit — all with one swing. Montgomery, a 37-year-old who had more than 300 career saves, announced his retirement after the season. ◆

— By John Lowe

INNING 9 STRIKE 2 KANSAS CITY 2
AT BAT 36 OUT 2 BALL 2 DETROIT 8

The last pitch: With an assist from catcher Brad Ausmus, Detroit's Todd Jones struck out Kansas City's Carlos Beltran at 7:07 p.m.

GABRIEL B. TAIT

> **"I was hoping it would be a strikeout. I wanted to get the ball. I didn't want to keep it for myself, obviously, but I wanted to get the putout — be the last person to touch a ball in play at Tiger Stadium. It's not something anybody's going to remember, but I'll remember."**
>
> – Brad Ausmus, Tigers catcher, on the game-ending strikeout

OVER IN A FLASH

More than 100 years of baseball at The Corner, and the end came in a flash — the flash from hundreds of cameras in the grandstands, the flash of one last pitch darting beyond a batter's reach.

With two out and two strikes on Carlos Beltran in the ninth inning, relief pitcher Todd Jones threw a curveball in the dirt that the Kansas City slugger flailed at for strike three. It was the last pitch of the last at-bat in the last major league game at baseball's oldest address.

"I guess the flashes got him or something like that," said Jones, speculating that Beltran might not have seen the pitch as well as the 43,356 fans in the stands did.

The end came at 7:07 p.m., when Jones, who had fired four straight fastballs to Beltran, threw the finishing hook. The ball was scooped by Tigers catcher Brad Ausmus, who tagged Beltran and then gave the ball to Bryan Schmakel.

Bryan Schmakel? The 19-year-old son of Tigers clubhouse manager Jim Schmakel had the

KIRTHMON F. DOZIER

Todd Jones struck a pose after striking out the last batter.

honor of collecting the balls taken out of the game to be preserved for posterity.

"Just being out there, you could feel it was something special," said Schmakel, a University of Dayton student who grew up in Toledo but nonetheless considered Tiger Sta-

dium his home park. He delivered the last ball, one of 20 he retrieved from the game, to his dad for safekeeping. For Schmakel, it was a baseball dream come true, as it was for Jones, who made no secret of his desire to pitch in the final game.

When Jones, the club's closer, reached the mound in the ninth inning, he found out just how pumped up he was. "I couldn't really get a good feel for what was going on out there," he said. "I had to calm myself down. I was just trying to throw it somewhere near Brad."

Then there were those camera flashes — "when you come set, and as soon as you go, all the cameras go," said Jones, who quickly retired the first two hitters in the inning. Then he composed himself enough to absorb the moment, one that no other pitcher would ever experience.

"I stepped off the back of the mound and took a look around," Jones said. "I just tried to soak it in a little bit because we had a good cushion, we had two outs and I had 0-2. If I wasn't going to do it then, I wasn't going to do it."

Jones maintained his composure during the last at-bat. "I was trying to not overstep my bounds," he said. "Just let the moment happen. I would have liked to do more, but this place doesn't need me. I just fulfilled the end. They had to have somebody out there. I'm just honored it was me." ◆

– *By David A. Markiewicz*

ALONG CAME JONES

Todd Jones, who was on the mound for the last out at The Corner, wrote about the finale from a player's point of view:

I haven't been here long — since December 1996. I knew then about the closing of Tiger Stadium. I thought, so what? I had just come from Houston, where we were trying to sell the concept of a new stadium, so it was old hat. That next week was TigerFest, our annual fan festival at Cobo Hall. All I heard was wait till Opening Day. When it came, I couldn't believe my eyes. It was 2 degrees, we were playing the Twins, and we were already under .500. The place was sold out and buzzing.

From that day on I wanted to know why — why this place is so special to everybody I've ever talked to. So I began to ask around. I don't care what anyone says, if you want to learn Tiger Stadium history, go to Nemo's and the Designated Hatter. I would go and just listen. I started to learn of Kell, Kaline, Greenberg, '68, '84 (35-5 start), Newhouser, the Babe's 700th homer, Lou Gehrig's streak ending, and so on. I learned about the overhang in rightfield. I learned that the seats over the Cheez-It sign are closer to home plate than shortstop is. And who could forget the bullpen, which is more like a submarine? Even though Al Kaline hasn't roamed rightfield for more than 20 years, it's still Kaline's Corner.

Now we have to close her

down. People know it's time, but it's not easy. We are the lucky few, this generation of Tigers. We get to close Tiger Stadium. But I have learned we are just an extension of you. I think all of us understand what this place means to you. We have seen it all this year. Fans come to see her one last time. After our games, people have to be asked to leave. I've seen hundreds of people reach over the rail for handfuls of dirt. I've seen people leave teary-eyed. That really makes

don't think we don't. After all, this is history.

Tiger Stadium opened April 20, 1912, and hardly anyone knew because the Titanic sank a few days earlier. Tiger Stadium will close Sept. 27, 1999, and because we had such a miserable season, not many will know outside of Detroit. It's kind of ironic. I'm really disgusted we couldn't shut this place down with a playoff or World Series game. She deserved to go out like that. Instead, she will go out like

Jones before the game: "We know what this place means to you."

RICHARD LEE

me stop and think.

We have signed everything you can imagine — scorebooks, balls, shirts, jerseys — just because we will be the last team to play in Tiger Stadium. We know we just represent the final chapter of a 100-year-old story. The guys won't tell you, but they are excited. We all want to play that last game to say we did it. We all have our mementos from the stadium —

she came in — not much fanfare except to us.

The '99 Tigers are honored to play the last game. Because we know what this place means to you, we will step lightly that last day because we certainly don't deserve such an honor. But I have a feeling we won't take those steps alone. You'll take them with us.

Thank you, Michigan and Trumbull. ◆

FINAL TIGERS LINEUP

LF
LUIS POLONIA
Wore Gibson's No. 23

C
BRAD AUSMUS
Wore Freehan's No. 11

1B
TONY CLARK
Wore Greenberg's No. 5

3B
DEAN PALMER
Wore Kell's No. 21

2B
DAMION EASLEY
Wore Gehringer's No. 2

RF
KARIM GARCIA
Wore Kaline's No. 6

CF
GABE KAPLER
Wore no number, just like Cobb

DH
ROBERT FICK
Wore Norm Cash's No. 25

SS
DEIVI CRUZ
Wore Trammell's No. 3

P
BRIAN MOEHLER
Wore Morris' No. 47

ALL-TIME TIGERS TEAM
(VOTED BY FANS)

OF
TY COBB
1905-26

OF
AL KALINE
1953-74

OF
KIRK GIBSON
1979-87
1993-95

1B
HANK GREENBERG
1933-46

2B
CHARLIE GEHRINGER
1924-42

3B
GEORGE KELL
1946-52

SS
ALAN TRAMMELL
1977-96

C
BILL FREEHAN
1961, 1963-76

RHP
JACK MORRIS
1977-90

LHP
HAL NEWHOUSER
1939-53

LHP
MICKEY LOLICH
1963-75

RP
JOHN HILLER
1965-70
1972-80

MGR
SPARKY ANDERSON
1979-95

KANSAS CITY	ab	r	h	rbi	bb	so	avg.
Febles 2b	4	0	1	0	0	1	.262
b-Pose ph	1	0	0	0	0	1	.285
Sanchez ss	5	0	2	0	0	0	.298
Beltran cf	4	1	3	0	1	1	.293
Dye rf	3	0	1	0	1	1	.293
Sweeney 1b	4	0	1	0	0	2	.323
Randa 3b	4	0	1	1	0	0	.317
Quinn lf	3	1	1	1	1	0	.340
Giambi dh	4	0	0	0	0	3	.286
Kreuter c	4	0	1	0	0	1	.225
Totals	36	2	11	2	3	10	

DETROIT	ab	r	h	rbi	bb	so	avg.
Polonia lf	3	1	2	1	0	0	.315
a-Jefferies ph	1	0	0	0	0	0	.200
Bartee cf	1	0	0	0	0	0	.188
Ausmus c	3	0	1	0	1	1	.279
Clark 1b	4	0	0	0	0	0	.279
Palmer 3b	3	1	2	0	1	0	.258
Easley 2b	3	2	3	0	0	0	.271
Garcia rf-lf	3	2	1	2	1	0	.237
Kapler cf-rf	3	1	1	0	1	0	.241
Fick dh	2	1	1	5	1	0	.219
Cruz ss	4	0	0	0	0	0	.280
Totals	30	8	11	8	5	1	

KANSAS CITY		011 000 000 –	2 11 1
DETROIT		110 002 04x –	8 11 0

a-grounded out for Polonia in the 7th. b-struck out for Febles in the 9th.
E: Dye (5). **LOB:** Kansas City 10, Detroit 5. **2B:** Beltran (27), Palmer (24), Easley (30). **HR:** Fick (3) off Montgomery; Garcia (13) off Suppan; Quinn (6) off Moehler; Polonia (8) off Suppan. **RBI:** Randa (81), Quinn (17), Polonia (30), Garcia 2 (29), Fick 5 (10). **SB:** Kapler (11). **CS:** Palmer (3). **S:** Easley. **SF:** Fick. **GIDP:** Sweeney, Randa, Clark.
Runners left in scoring position: Kansas City 4 (Randa 3, Giambi), Detroit 2 (Cruz 2). **Runners moved up:** Cruz.
DP: Kansas City 2 (Sanchez and Sweeney), (Dye and Sweeney); Detroit 2 (Palmer, Easley and Clark), (Easley, Cruz and Clark).

KANSAS CITY	ip	h	r	er	bb	so	np	avg.
Suppan (L 10-11)	5 1/3	8	4	4	3	1	94	4.51
Morman	1 2/3	0	0	0	1	0	19	4.10
Montgomery	1	3	4	4	1	0	17	6.93

DETROIT	ip	h	r	er	bb	so	np	avg.
Moehler (W 10-16)	6	9	2	2	2	5	109	5.04
Cordero	1/3	2	0	0	1	1	16	3.50
Brocall	1 2/3	0	0	0	0	2	16	2.63
Jones	1	0	0	0	0	2	10	3.90

Inherited runners-scored: Morman 1-0, Brocall 3-0.
IBB: off Montgomery (Garcia) 1.
T: 2:58. **A:** 43,356.
Umpires: Home, Roe; 1b, Reed; 2b, Merrill; 3b, Reynolds.

Dean Palmer was out at home in the bottom of the eighth, and the next batter — with the bases loaded — was Robert Fick.

KIRTHMON F. DOZIER

PLAY-BY-PLAY

FIRST INNING

ROYALS: Febles flied to centerfielder Kapler. Sanchez singled to right-center. Beltran singled to left, Sanchez to second. Dye walked, Sanchez to third, Beltran to second. Sweeney struck out. Randa lined to second baseman Easley. **0 runs, 2 hits, 0 errors, 3 left. Tigers 0, Royals 0.**

TIGERS: Polonia homered to right-center on 1-2 count. Ausmus singled to center. Clark grounded into a double play, shortstop Sanchez to first baseman Sweeney, Ausmus out. Palmer walked on a full count. Palmer was caught stealing, catcher Kreuter to second baseman Febles. **1 run, 2 hits, 0 errors, 0 left. Tigers 1, Royals 0.**

SECOND INNING

ROYALS: Quinn homered to left on 2-2 count. Giambi struck out. Kreuter flied to centerfielder Kapler. Febles singled to short. Sanchez lined to rightfielder Garcia. **1 run, 2 hits, 0 errors, 1 left. Tigers 1, Royals 1.**

TIGERS: Easley doubled to third. Garcia grounded out, first baseman Sweeney unassisted, Easley to third. Kapler walked on a full count. Fick hit sacrifice fly to rightfielder Dye, scoring Easley. Kapler stole second. Cruz grounded out, shortstop Sanchez to first baseman Sweeney. **1 run, 1 hit, 0 errors, 1 left. Tigers 2, Royals 1.**

THIRD INNING

ROYALS: Beltran singled to right. Dye singled to right, Beltran to second. Sweeney grounded into a double play, third baseman Palmer to second baseman Easley to first baseman Clark, Beltran to third. Randa singled to center, scoring Beltran. Quinn walked, Randa to second. Giambi grounded out, first baseman Clark to pitcher Moehler. **1 run, 3 hits, 0 errors, 2 left. Tigers 2, Royals 2.**

TIGERS: Polonia singled to third. Ausmus struck out. Clark flied to leftfielder Quinn. Palmer flied to centerfielder Beltran. **0 runs, 1 hit, 0 errors, 1 left. Tigers 2, Royals 2.**

FOURTH INNING

ROYALS: Kreuter grounded out, first baseman Clark to pitcher Moehler. Febles grounded out, first baseman Clark to pitcher Moehler. Sanchez lined to rightfielder Garcia. **0 runs, 0 hits, 0 errors, 0 left. Tigers 2, Royals 2.**

TIGERS: Easley singled to left. Garcia grounded into fielder's choice, first baseman Sweeney to shortstop Sanchez. Kapler grounded into fielder's choice, shortstop Sanchez to second baseman Febles. Fick walked, Kapler to second. Cruz flied to centerfielder Beltran. **0 runs, 1 hit, 0 errors, 2 left. Tigers 2, Royals 2.**

FIFTH INNING

ROYALS: Beltran doubled to center. Dye popped to rightfielder Garcia. Sweeney struck out. Randa grounded out, third baseman Palmer to first baseman Clark. **0 runs, 1 hit, 0 errors, 1 left. Tigers 2, Royals 2.**

TIGERS: Polonia grounded out, first baseman Sweeney unassisted. Ausmus flied to centerfielder Beltran. Clark grounded out, first baseman Sweeney to pitcher Suppan. **0 runs, 0 hits, 0 errors, 0 left. Tigers 2, Royals 2.**

SIXTH INNING

ROYALS: Quinn lined to rightfielder Garcia. Giambi struck out. Kreuter singled to center. Febles struck out. **0 runs, 1 hit, 0 errors, 1 left. Tigers 2, Royals 2.**

TIGERS: Palmer singled to third. Easley sacrificed, catcher Kreuter to second baseman Febles, Palmer to second. Garcia homered to left on a 1-1 count. Kapler singled to left. Morman pitching. Fick lined into a double play, rightfielder Dye to first baseman Sweeney. **2 runs, 3 hits, 0 errors, 0 left. Tigers 4, Royals 2.**

SEVENTH INNING

ROYALS: Cordero pitching. Sanchez singled to center. Beltran walked on a full count, Sanchez to second. Dye struck out. Sweeney singled to right, Sanchez to third, Beltran to second. Brocail pitching. Randa grounded into a double play, second baseman Easley to shortstop Cruz to first baseman Clark. **0 runs, 2 hits, 0 errors, 2 left. Tigers 4, Royals 2.**

TIGERS: Cruz grounded out, third baseman Randa to first baseman Sweeney. Jefferies, pinch-hitting for Polonia, grounded out, shortstop Sanchez to first baseman Sweeney. Ausmus walked on four pitches. Clark fouled to rightfielder Dye. **0 runs, 0 hits, 0 errors, 1 left. Tigers 4, Royals 2.**

EIGHTH INNING

ROYALS: Bartee in centerfield. Garcia to leftfield. Kapler to rightfield. Quinn flied to centerfielder Bartee. Giambi struck out. Kreuter struck out. **0 runs, 0 hits, 0 errors, 0 left. Tigers 4, Royals 2.**

TIGERS: Montgomery pitching. Palmer doubled to left. Easley singled to right, Palmer to third. On Dye's error, Easley to second. Garcia intentionally walked. Kapler grounded into fielder's choice, pitcher Montgomery to catcher Kreuter, Easley to third, Garcia to second. Fick homered to right on the first pitch. Cruz grounded out, third baseman Randa to first baseman Sweeney. Bartee grounded out, shortstop Sanchez to first baseman Sweeney. **4 runs, 3 hits, 1 error, 0 left. Tigers 8, Royals 2.**

NINTH INNING

ROYALS: Jones pitching. Pose, pinch-hitting for Febles, struck out. Sanchez lined to second baseman Easley. Beltran struck out. **0 runs, 0 hits, 0 errors, 0 left. Tigers 8, Royals 2.**

FIRST...

■ **Boos:** For Tigers owner Mike Ilitch, probably because he engineered the move to Comerica Park. Gov. John Engler and baseball commissioner Bud Selig received the same reception.

■ **Bit of welcome hyperbole:** Engler called Al Kaline the best rightfielder ever. Baseball historians might be partial to Babe Ruth or Hank Aaron, but if there were any such historians in the park, they wisely kept quiet.

■ **Ovation:** For Kaline, adding to his record total of Tiger Stadium ovations.

■ **Pitch (ceremonial):** From Billy Rogell, 94, a shortstop for the Tigers in 1930-39. Rogell's toss was caught barehanded by Brad Ausmus.

■ **Pitch (actual):** From Brian Moehler to Carlos Febles at 4:09 p.m. Febles flied to centerfielder Gabe Kapler. Unlike Ausmus, Kapler used his glove.

■ **Hit:** By the game's second batter, Rey Sanchez, on a 2-2 pitch, a shot to right-center.

■ **Tigers hit:** Luis Polonia led off the bottom of the first by sending a 1-2 pitch over the 415 sign in right-centerfield. ◆

> ► **TIGERS' FINAL RECORD AT THE CORNER (1912-1999)** **3764-3090** (.549) ◄
>
> Plus 19 ties – total games played: 6,873

LAST...

■ **National anthem:** Performed by the Mosaic Youth Theatre.

■ **Exchange of lineup cards:** By Hall of Famers George Brett and Kaline, Nos. 5 and 6, for the Royals and Tigers.

■ **Argument with an umpire:** Tigers manager Larry Parrish disputed a call at home plate in the eighth, but he was subdued.

■ **Roof shot:** Robert Fick hit his first career grand slam in the eighth inning — it landed on the rightfield roof and bounced back onto the field.

■ **Curtain call:** After chants of "Fick! Fick! Fick!" the rookie obliged.

■ **Out:** Carlos Beltran struck out swinging against Todd Jones, ending the game and the era.

J. KYLE KEENER

■ **Wave:** With two out in the bottom of the seventh and Tony Clark of the Tigers batting, the crowd gave one of the most spirited waves in years. The wave was popularized at The Corner in 1984, and it will never be the same — none of baseball's new parks can match the two-tier, around-the-park wave of Tiger Stadium. ◆

SAY IT AIN'T SO

You'll have to subtract about 15 feet from your Tiger Stadium memories. The distance from home plate to centerfield at The Corner wasn't 440 feet — even though the Tigers had for decades displayed that distinctively Detroit depth on the centerfield wall.

The real distance from the plate to the wall in dead center was about 425 feet, Tigers president John McHale revealed during spring training 2000. However, that still made it the deepest dimension in the majors.

"I can't remember when we discovered this," McHale said. "We've had various measurements of the park re-taken in recent years to help us in our thought process for Comerica Park. We didn't do a step-off — we did an actual measurement."

So upon what was the 440 sign based?

"I don't know how to explain it, or what it means," McHale said. ◆

LONG GONE TIGER STADIUM HOME RUNS (1912-1999)

FIRST:
Del Pratt   St. Louis Browns   May 5, 1912

TOTAL: **11,113**

Tigers: **5,574**   Visitors: **5,539**

MEN ON BASE:

0: **6,180**   1: **3,315**   2: **1,337**   3: **281**

Pinch hit: **224**. Leadoff: **177**. Extra innings: **198**. Inside park: **131**

Right-handed: **6,245**   Left-handed: **4,868**

TOTALS

#	Player	HR		#	Player	HR
1	Al Kaline	226		56	Al Simmons	32
2	Norm Cash	212		57	Joe DiMaggio	30
3	Hank Greenberg	187			Dean Palmer	30
4	Lou Whitaker	146			Harvey Kuenn	30
5	Rudy York	140			Frank Bolling	30
6	Cecil Fielder	130		61	Eddie Yost	29
7	Willie Horton	127		62	Bob Nieman	27
8	Dick McAuliffe	107			Johnny Groth	27
9	Lance Parrish	102			Ron LeFlore	27
10	Bill Freehan	100			Champ Summers	27
11	Alan Trammell	97		66	Roger Maris	26
12	Kirk Gibson	95			Boog Powell	26
13	Charlie Gehringer	92			Gus Zernial	26
14	Jim Northrup	90			Fred Lynn	26
15	Chet Lemon	85			Walt Dropo	26
16	Charlie Maxwell	84		71	Frank House	25
	Harry Heilmann	84			Pete Fox	25
18	Vic Wertz	81		73	Vern Stephens	24
19	Travis Fryman	79			Minnie Minoso	24
20	Rocky Colavito	75			Jim Delsing	24
	Darrell Evans	75			Mike Heath	24
22	Tony Clark	65			Bill Bruton	24
23	Mickey Stanley	62			Dave Bergman	24
24	Mickey Tettleton	61		79	Bob Johnson	23
25	Babe Ruth	60			Larry Doby	23
26	Bobby Higginson	59			Reggie Jackson	23
27	Ray Boone	58			Mark McGwire	23
28	Steve Kemp	56			Bud Souchock	23
29	Ted Williams	55			Don Demeter	23
30	Jimmie Foxx	52		85	Lou Gehrig	22
	Pat Mullin	52			Joe Gordon	22
32	Gates Brown	50			George Brett	22
	Jason Thompson	50			Earl Torgeson	22
34	Aurelio Rodriguez	47			Dale Alexander	22
	Don Wert	47			Jake Wood	22
36	Mike Higgins	44		91	Eddie Robinson	21
37	Roy Cullenbine	43			Graig Nettles	21
	Damion Easley	43			Tom Tresh	21
39	Mickey Mantle	42		94	Eddie Murray	20
	John Wockenfuss	42			Cal Ripken	20
41	Rusty Staub	41			Frank Howard	20
	Tom Brookens	41			Aaron Robinson	20
43	Rob Deer	40			Bobby Veach	20
44	Hoot Evers	39			Richie Hebner	20
	Larry Herndon	39		100	Tommy Henrich	19
46	Yogi Berra	37			Mickey Vernon	19
	Goose Goslin	37			Jackie Jensen	19
48	Carl Yastrzemski	36			Dwight Evans	19
49	Harmon Killebrew	35			Red Kress	19
	Ben Oglivie	35			Charlie Keller	19
	Gee Walker	35			Gus Triandos	19
52	Marty McManus	34			Jerry Priddy	19
	Matt Nokes	34			John Grubb	19
	Dick Wakefield	34			Bill Tuttle	19
55	Tony Phillips	33				

MOST BY VISITORS (Career)

#	Player	HR
1	Babe Ruth	60
2	Ted Williams	55
3	Jimmie Foxx	52
4	Mickey Mantle	42
5	Yogi Berra	37
6	Carl Yastrzemski	36
7	Harmon Killebrew	35
8	Joe DiMaggio	30
9	Roger Maris	26
	Boog Powell	26
11	Vern Stephens	24
	Minnie Minoso	24
13	Bob Johnson	23
	Larry Doby	23
	Reggie Jackson	23
	Mark McGwire	23
17	Al Simmons	22
	Lou Gehrig	22
	Joe Gordon	22
	George Brett	22
21	Eddie Robinson	21
	Graig Nettles	21
23	Vic Wertz	20
	Eddie Murray	20
	Cal Ripken	20

MOST BY TIGERS (Career)

#	Player	HR
1	Al Kaline	226
2	Norm Cash	211
3	Hank Greenberg	187
4	Lou Whitaker	146
5	Rudy York	139
6	Cecil Fielder	127
7	Willie Horton	124
8	Dick McAuliffe	107
9	Bill Freehan	100
10	Lance Parrish	98
11	Alan Trammell	97
12	Kirk Gibson	95
13	Charlie Gehringer	92
14	Jim Northrup	87
15	Harry Heilmann	84
16	Charlie Maxwell	83
17	Chet Lemon	82
18	Travis Fryman	77
19	Darrell Evans	75
20	Rocky Colavito	67
21	Tony Clark	65
22	Mickey Stanley	62
23	Vic Wertz	61
24	Bobby Higginson	59
25	Mickey Tettleton	58

J. KYLE KEENER

Al Kaline hit more homers at The Corner than any other player.

MOST BY A TIGER IN A SEASON

#	Player	Year	HR
1	Hank Greenberg	1938	39
2	Hank Greenberg	1946	29
3	Hank Greenberg	1940	27
	Cecil Fielder	1991	27
5	Hank Greenberg	1937	25
	Norm Cash	1962	25
	Cecil Fielder	1990	25

MOST BY A VISITOR IN A SEASON

#	Player	Year	HR
1	Jimmie Foxx	1932	9
2	Jimmie Foxx	1937	7
	Yogi Berra	1951	7
	Gus Zernial	1953	7
	Mickey Mantle	1956	7
	Roger Maris	1958	7
	Gary Geiger	1963	7
	Mark McGwire	1987	7

BALLPARKS WITH MOST HOMERS

#	Ballpark	HR
1	Tiger Stadium	11,113
2	Wrigley Field	10,058
3	Yankee Stadium	9,530
4	Fenway Park	9,407
5	Sportsman's Park	8,268
6	Shibe Park	6,965
7	Cleveland Stadium	6,659
8	Polo Grounds	6,657
9	Comiskey Park	6,250
10	County Stadium	5,677

Source: David Vincent, Society for American Baseball Research

ERIC SEALS

**Engaging:
During the game,
Joshua Rubin
popped the
question and
Mikki Liebeman
said yes.
Below: Dave Beck
and Debi Clymer
cherished
the closing
ceremonies.**

KIRTHMON F. DOZIER

Two of the finale's 43,356 fans found quiet time amidst the clamor.

Craig Mehl of Warren was on top of the world after snagging a foul ball in the eighth inning, but the closing ceremonies brought him back to Earth as time ran out on The Corner.

FIELD OF DREAMS

By Nicholas J. Cotsonika

The closing ceremonies were an emotional mix of tears, jeers and cheers — an hour-long requiem for a lost loved one.

As soon as the game ended, head groundskeeper Heather Nabozny and members of her crew surrounded home plate. Using a miner's pickax, Charlie McGee unearthed the 75-pound treasure at 7:13 p.m.

A few fans dashed onto the field, but a police perimeter kept things orderly as Ernie Harwell began a somber, final program. With music from the movie "Field of Dreams" playing in the background, Harwell read a brief history of The Corner, where baseball was played for 104 years. Then he introduced a film, which played on the centerfield scoreboard.

Images of Al Kaline appeared, then Ty Cobb, Sam Crawford, Hughie Jennings and Harry Heilmann. Tigers' Hall of Famers were honored: Heinie Manush, Mickey Cochrane, Charlie Gehringer, Hank Greenberg, Hal Newhouser, George Kell and, of course, Harwell.

The crowd was hushed until Willie Horton spoke: "Tiger Stadium is life, as far as I'm concerned," and then they cheered. Sparky Anderson said: "I'm going to put it in my mind, so it will always be there." More cheers. The film faded out, showing Tiger Stadium in the twilight. Louder still.

And then the players appeared — the great and the not-so-great, the ➤➤

Final swings at The Corner fell to groundskeeper Charlie McGee, who used a pickax before hoisting home plate.

Opposite page: Lou Whitaker and Alan Trammell, teammates for 19 seasons, together at The Corner one last time.

GABRIEL B. TAIT (2)

CORNER TO COPA

beloved and the beleaguered, from every era, streaming out from the gate in centerfield and taking their positions in full uniform. One-by-one they came, some riding in carts.

The Bird, Mark Fidrych, was first. Still lanky, still gangly, still goofy, he sprinted to the mound, dropped to one knee — as he did, famously, in the 1970s — and placed some dirt in a plastic bag.

Bill Freehan was next, then Dick McAuliffe, Dave Bergman, Mickey Stanley (who took his position in center, not short) and Horton, crying and pumping his fists.

"When we were getting ready to line up, I had a little prayer off by myself," said Horton, who grew up in Detroit. "It was joy for my grandkids and sadness for myself. I tell you, the feeling is unreal."

Members of the 1999 Tigers were in awe. Bobby Higginson took home videos. Rookie Robert Fick looked like a curious kid, crouched on his knees in the grass.

Kirk Gibson came out, jumping and whooping, then Cecil Fielder, Kaline, and Lou Whitaker and Alan Trammell, together as always. "We said we were just going to run out there and do what was natural," Trammell said.

The players made a long line from the 440-foot sign in centerfield, the deepest in the bigs, to home plate. The Tiger Stadium flag was lowered, then passed, player-to-player, until 1930s pitcher Eldon Auker presented it to turn-of-the-century catcher Brad Ausmus.

"Never forget us," Auker said.

A few minutes after 8, home plate arrived at the Tigers' new home, Comerica Park, which had been booed at every mention. Back at The Corner, players threw souvenir balls into the stands. Fans leaned over the railing and scooped up dirt with plastic cups. The lights dimmed. Harwell said farewell, his golden voice breaking.

"Tonight," he said, "we say good-bye. … Farewell, old friend Tiger Stadium. We will remember."

At 8:19, the scoreboard went dark.

At 8:45, a team photo was taken.

By 9, the stands were empty. Silence. Among the last to leave were a few fans who hung a banner from the right-centerfield overhang, a banner that spoke for a sad city:

"Today, there is crying in baseball. So long, old friend." ◆

Sparky Anderson, recovering from heart bypass surgery, sent greetings from his California home.

RICHARD LEE

SPARKY SPEAKS

"If you have any understanding of sports in Detroit, you'll know that today is probably the greatest sporting event in the history of Detroit. This will go down in history as the greatest moment of sports in all of Detroit."

CAREER HIGHLIGHTS

► Elected to the Baseball Hall of Fame on Feb. 29, 2000.
► Became Tigers manager June 12, 1979. First game in uniform was June 14. Last game was Oct. 1, 1995.
► Led 1984 Tigers to club-record 104 wins.
► First manager to win a World Series in both leagues (Cincinnati, 1975-76; Detroit, 1984).

OVERALL	WON-LOST	PCT.
NL total	863-586	.596
AL total	1331-1248	.516
Total	2194-1834	.545
Playoffs	18-9	.667
World Series	16-12	.571

**First out of the gate among Tigers old-timers was
The Bird, Mark Fidrych, who assumed a familiar
perch on the pitcher's mound.**

HONOR ROLL

Billy Rogell	1930-39
Eldon Auker	1933-38
Jake Wade	1936-38
Harry Eisenstat	1938-39
Les Mueller	1941, 1945
Virgil Trucks	1941-43, 1945-52, 1956
Hal White	1941-43, 1946-52
John McHale Sr.	1943-45, 1947-48
Jimmy Outlaw	1943-49
Red Borom	1944-45
Eddie Mayo	1944-48
Art Houtteman	1945-50, 1952-53
Ed Mierkowicz	1945, 1947-48
Billy Pierce	1945, 1948
George Kell	1946-52
Joe Ginsberg	1948, 1950-53
Don Lund	1949, 1952-54
Ray Herbert	1950-51, 1953-54
Dick Kryhoski	1950-51
Billy Hoeft	1952-59
Reno Bertoia	1953-58, 1961-62
Ray Boone	1953-58
Steve Gromek	1953-57
Al Kaline	1953-74
Jim Bunning	1955-63
Charlie Maxwell	1955-62
Eddie Yost	1959-60
Dick McAuliffe	1960-73
Bill Freehan	1961, 1963-76
Jake Wood	1961-67
Gates Brown	1963-75
Willie Horton	1963-77
Mickey Lolich	1963-75
Don Wert	1963-70
Jim Northrup	1964-74
Mickey Stanley	1964-78
John Hiller	1965-70, 1972-80
Dick Tracewski	1966-69
Earl Wilson	1966-70
Jim Price	1967-71
Aurelio Rodriguez	1971-79
Ron LeFlore	1974-79

GATES
BROWN
1963-75

J. KYLE KEENER

MICKEY
LOLICH
1963-75

"It's always been my most favorite ballpark, and I've played in quite a few – Yankee Stadium, Fenway, Comiskey. When I first saw it, I was in love with it, and I still feel the same way about it now."

– Dick McAuliffe
(greeting Lolich)

John Wockenfuss	1974-83
Mark Fidrych	1976-80
Jason Thompson	1976-80
Steve Kemp	1977-81
Jack Morris	1977-90
Lance Parrish	1977-86
Dave Rozema	1977-84
Alan Trammell	1977-96
Lou Whitaker	1977-95
Milt Wilcox	1977-85
Tom Brookens	1979-88
Kirk Gibson	1979-87, 1993-95
Dan Petry	1979-87, 1990-91
Larry Herndon	1982-88
Chet Lemon	1982-90
Dave Bergman	1984-92
Darrell Evans	1984-88
Guillermo Hernandez	1984-89
Frank Tanana	1985-92
Mike Henneman	1987-95
Cecil Fielder	1990-96

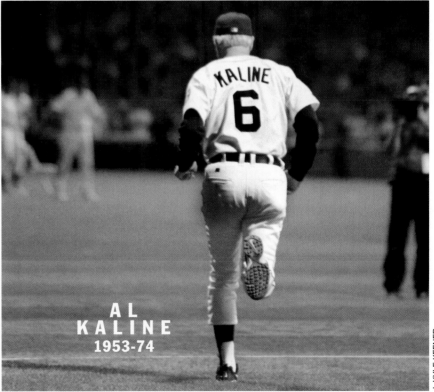

AL
KALINE
1953-74

"It was time for us. We weren't playing for individual goals, we were playing to win a championship. That (1984) was an awesome time."

CHET LEMON
1982-90

J. KYLE KEENER (2)

JACK MORRIS
1977-90

"My very first start was replacing Mark Fidrych, who was injured, and 45,000 people booed me because they wanted to see The Bird pitch. That was something I had to get over in a hurry when I was a young boy. Fortunately, we went out and won the game. They cheered me at the end."

GABRIEL B. TAIT

ALAN
TRAMMELL
1977-96

LOU
WHITAKER
1977-95

"I'm very proud to say that I played my entire career here.
I've been part of this place for over 20 years, and, hey, I loved
every minute of it. ... I'm going to take my nameplate on my locker.
Other than that, I'm taking memories."

– Alan Trammell

JULIAN H. GONZALEZ

LANCE
PARRISH
1977-86

BILL
FREEHAN
1961, 1963-76

JIM
PRICE
1967-71

J. KYLE KEENER

Kirk Gibson, voted by fans to the all-time team, was in the middle of the lineup once again.

GABRIEL B. TAIT

CARLOS OSORIO / Associated Press

Jake Wade, a pitcher who was born a few days before Navin Field
opened in 1912, was back on the mound for the much-photographed finale.

Fans cheered as a final team photo was taken; Mark Fidrych, Gates Brown, Jake Wood and Earl Wilson cheered the occasion, as well.

> **"Brad, take this flag to Comerica Park, your new home,
> and take with it the boyhood dreams, the perseverance
> and the competitive desire it takes to become a Detroit Tiger."**
>
> – Eldon Auker

Capping a star-spangled night, the flag that flew over the finale was passed from player to player until a pitcher from the 1930s, Eldon Auker, delivered it to modern-day catcher Brad Ausmus.

JULIAN H. GONZALEZ

THOSE WERE THE DAYS

By Mitch Albom

Look, there's your father, sitting in the rightfield seats, handing you a hot dog and telling you to be careful, don't get mustard all over your shirt.

And over there, near the third base line, there's your grandma, holding her little pencil and writing names delicately in her scorecard, "Kaline, RF, Horton, LF, Freehan, C… ."

And out there, in the bleachers, isn't that your first girlfriend, looking the way she did back then, her hair in a ponytail, her eyes feigning interest as you point out the players and proudly quote their statistics?

Didn't you see them all there, taking their place with the rest of the remembered, the living and the ghosts, the players and managers, the umpires and owners, all of whom came to wave good-bye to an 87-year-old fading blue palace called Tiger Stadium?

Didn't they gather early at The Corner, gazing up fondly at the light towers and the peeling-white walls?

Didn't they come through the turnstiles and immediately inhale, sniffing the smells of history mixed with sausage grease?

Didn't they roar for the old players who gathered at home plate

Before the flag was lowered, young and old gathered at The Corner as they have for 104 seasons.

before the national anthem?

Didn't they laugh and point when Mark Fidrych ran out to the pitcher's mound and scooped up a last bag of dirt?

Didn't they get a chill when the great Al Kaline, speaking for everyone who ever wore a Tigers uniform, said, I "again find myself humbled"?

Didn't they jump up, the way all baseball fans jump up, when the first pitch was smacked toward centerfield — Could it be a homer? Will it be a homer? — and didn't they applaud when it came down in the glove of a Tigers centerfielder?

"You remember the first time you ever saw this stadium?" a 70-year-old man was asked on this farewell day.

"The first time? Oh, yeah," he said. "I was in high school, and I cut class and sneaked down here with a friend. And of the 50,000 people here, who should we run into? His mother! We didn't know what to say."

The 70-year-old man laughed. His eyes got that hazy look. Just for a moment he was by himself, gazing toward the outfield. His name is Mike Ilitch. He owns the team. That was his friend out there, in the bleachers, did you see him? The red-faced teenager trying to explain himself to Mom?

Look, there's your pal from the old neighborhood, grinning as his hand dives into your popcorn.

And over there's your uncle, waiting in his Chevrolet, parked by

the church where he said he'd meet you after the game.

There, in the upper deck, aren't those your schoolmates on Safety Patrol Day, having made the long bus trip down from northern Michigan?

And down there, along the outfield wall, isn't that your kid sister leaning over the rail during batting practice, her big glove dangling from her too-small hand? "Hit one here!" she would squeal to the players. "Hit one here!"

Weren't they all there for the final game?

You ask why people cry when baseball stadiums close. This is why. Because some of us found our childhoods inside them.

And some of us left them there. ◆

HEALING OLD WOUNDS

Saying good-bye to The Corner didn't bring tears to all Detroiters, because the Tigers never connected well with the black community.

The team left a growing, influential segment of the populace feeling unwanted, and the stadium served as a symbol of that exclusion.

■ **Willie Horton:** "That '68 team has always been credited with helping bring the races together in the city the year after the riots. That might be one of the proudest achievements I ever had during my Tiger career. That might have been the first time the Tigers ever made that connection with the black community."

■ **Gates Brown:** "I have nothing but fond memories of my experiences with these guys and this organization, but I can certainly understand why a lot of people don't look upon this stadium as fondly as others. And the Tigers have only themselves to blame for that. They missed the chance to create that connection with the city. Maybe they can make up for that with the new park."

■ **Horton:** "The city has come a long way, and this team has come a long way back from when I used to sneak inside the stadium when I was 12. But I guess some memories are still too deep for some to put aside. I'm still a proud part of my old neighborhood, but I haven't had a lot of people in my neighborhood come up to me and tell me how much they're going to miss this old ballpark."

■ **Ron LeFlore:** "It's not that folks are mad over stuff that happened 50 or so years ago, but it's that they just don't care because they probably think the team doesn't care. And that's probably even sadder. Some wounds take longer to heal than others." ◆

– By Drew Sharp

MARY SCHROEDER

LAST BUS FROM THE CORNER

At the end of the amazing day, Todd Jones was floored.

Jones, the Tigers' closer who threw the last pitch at The Corner, slept in the clubhouse. He had planned to spend the night somewhere in Tiger Stadium, and when he couldn't find anyone to join him in a camp-out on the field, he opted for the couch in the manager's office.

But Jones, 6-feet-3, couldn't get comfortable and moved to the floor.

And he had company. Brian Moehler, the winning pitcher in the finale, slept on a mattress in the clubhouse.

The Tigers had planned to leave for the season's final trip soon after the game but postponed their departure until the next morning, prompting an overnight stay by Jones and Moehler.

The two went to dinner separately before returning to the yard. Jones had a hamburger at Nemo's — a neighborhood bar — and found the place bustling with people who didn't want to let go of the historic day.

"That kind of brought it all together, to see how important that game was to everybody," Jones said. He said at least 50 people expressed thanks or congratulations to him for the team having won the finale.

After Robert Fick's eighth-inning grand slam, Jones finished the 8-2 victory with a perfect ninth, ending it by whiffing Kansas City's Carlos Beltran amid a sea of flashbulbs.

"I knew the flashbulbs were going nuts, but I didn't realize there were that many," Jones said after

seeing a replay of the final out. "On each pitch after there were two out, there were more and more and more."

Immediately after the game, Jones watched a tape of the final inning. For one of the few times in his career, he couldn't remember the details of his outing. He was in a fog, with so many things on his mind.

As Moehler layed his head on the clubhouse pillow that night, he too thought about the flashbulb-filled final out. "I'll never forget it," Moehler said. "I've never been in the playoffs, but I can't imagine it getting much better than that, as far as adrenaline and fans and the atmosphere.

"The postgame ceremony, as much as the game, was just incredible. It was a first-class effort by the organization and everyone in the front office. You could tell they had a rough week leading up to that, but they did a great job."

While Jones and Moehler were drifting off at Tiger Stadium, Luis Polonia lay awake on his couch, watching ESPN for five straight hours. The Tigers' 5-8 leadoff hitter saw several replays of his stunning, first-inning homer that carried over the 415 sign in right-center.

"I didn't think I'd gotten my arms extended, but I saw on the replay that I did," Polonia said. "I was just trying to make contact with two strikes." Polonia finally fell asleep about 4 a.m. Before long he was up, heading back to Tiger Stadium for the bus ride to the airport and the season-ending trip to Minnesota and Kansas City.

Not all the players would return to Detroit when the season ended. So as they congregated at the park in their street clothes that morning, it marked the final time that a Tigers team ever would be together at Tiger Stadium.

Then they got on the bus, and it pulled away from the ballpark.

The post-Tiger Stadium era had begun. ◆

– By John Lowe

ERNIE'S FAREWELL

Ladies and gentlemen, less than six months ago, we began a warm season of farewells, and with each passing day we came a little bit closer to this historic occasion.

The Lions, Joe Louis and Nelson Mandela. Six-thousand, eight-hundred and seventy-three regular-season games, 35 postseason contests and a trio of spectacular All-Star Games, Tiger Stadium has been home to this great game of baseball. But more than anything, it has been a cherished home to our memories.

Will you remember that last base hit? The last out? How about that last pitch? Or maybe it's the first time as a child when you saw that green, green grass that will forever be etched into your mind and soul.

Tonight, we say good-bye. But we will not forget. Open your eyes, look around and take a mental picture. Moments like this shall live on forever.

It's been 88 moving years at Michigan and Trumbull. The tradition built here shall endure along with the permanence of the Olde English D. But tonight we must say good-bye.

Farewell, old friend Tiger Stadium. We will remember.

KIRTHMON F. DOZIER

WE WILL REMEMBER

By Mitch Albom

We will remember the good and the bad: the long concession lines, the snarling hallway traffic, the girders that blocked our view, the rusty bleachers, the trough-like urinals in the men's bathrooms.

But mostly we will remember the rightfield porch that robbed outfielders of easy fly balls. (They stood helplessly underneath, gloves poised, and then — thwack! — a fan would walk off with a home run souvenir.)

The radio booth, where Ernie Harwell and Paul Carey and so many others plied their trade, behind home plate, hanging down like a pine cone, so close to the field that players could hear their names broadcast during their at-bats.

The flagpole, in dead center, which was in play if you hit it.

The dugout roofs, where a zealous fan nicknamed The Brow once danced.

The bleachers, at times loud, at times drunken, but always symbolic of a place where real fans could see a game without hooking into a corporate sales package.

We will remember when the site was Bennett Park, then Navin Field, then Briggs Stadium.

When the Tigers were no-hit in their first American League game.

When only 404 fans showed up.

When Ty Cobb got his 4,000th hit.

When Babe Ruth hit a 626-foot home run.

When Dizzy Dean shut out the Tigers to win a World Series for St. Louis.

When Lou Gehrig ended his Ironman streak.

When Hank Greenberg returned from four years in the Army and hit a home run in his first game back.

When fans danced in the streets after the Tigers won the World Series in 1968.

When Mark Fidrych talked to the ball and Kirk Gibson yelled at the skies and Frank Tanana's bubble gum flew from his mouth after he pitched a shutout that sent the Tigers to the 1987 playoffs.

We will remember the cheers, the beers, a national anthem, a scoreboard, a pennant, a hot dog, a Coke, a two-run double, a bases-loaded strikeout, a kid with a glove, an old man with a scorecard, sausage grease, caramel corn, rusted girders, peeling paint.

We will remember where Joe Louis fought a heavyweight fight, where the Lions played football, where the Three Tenors sang opera. We will never grow cold as long as we remember the warmth. We will never become jaded adults as long as we revel in youthful memories.

We will remember. ◆

Cradled by the young arms of pitchers Matt Anderson, Jeff Weaver and Francisco Cordero, home plate arrived at its new home, Comerica Park, about an hour after the final out.

THE END

APRIL 20, 1912 - SEPT. 27, 1999

J. KYLE KEENER

THE
BEGINNING
APRIL 11, 2000

THERE'S NO PLACE LIKE HOME

By Nicholas J. Cotsonika

As a new era dawned, fans could embrace the past while roaring into the future.

The sky was gray as dawn broke over Comerica Park. A hard snow fell. Not a light, flaky snow. A hard snow. The kind that stings your skin when the wind whips, that makes you wonder why you drove downtown to watch baseball in miserable 34-degree weather, Opening Day or not, Inaugural Game or not. And still the fans came early. The first few milled ⮞

KENT PHILLIPS

From on high, downtown Detroiters checked out the new neighbors. Inside, there was plenty new underfoot, including personalized bricks.

DAVID P. GILKEY

J. KYLE KEENER

around outside, along Woodward, hours before pitcher Brian Moehler began the Tigers' new era by throwing a strike at 1:18 p.m. They partied at the Hockeytown Cafe, tried desperately to find affordable parking near the Fox Theatre, stared at this place they had heard so much about but had never seen. They were excited.

Curious. Like little kids, they wanted to know what was inside. They wanted to unwrap this present. They couldn't wait to experience what was a full day of discovery, daydreaming and introspection for nearly every Detroiter from the owner to the last peanut guy.

The walk from Woodward along Montcalm to the park's home-plate gate was an uplifting experience if you're a baseball buff who has suffered in this city for so long. There were beautiful bricks and sculpted concrete tigers and, remarkably, the field.

Through the wrought-iron fence, from the street itself, came the first view. There was the great green grass. There were the seats, green again, similar to the kind Detroiters sat in long ago. Another peek, and there it was. Off in the distance, out toward centerfield, there was that skyline panorama that was supposed to be the stadium's signature.

The anticipation was intense. Time to go inside.

Walking around the concourse was like touring a mansion. So much room. So much to see. Not everything had been finished, so there were still construction zones and "Coming Soon" signs posted everywhere. But mostly all the bells and whistles that cost $300 million were there, ready to be inspected, enjoyed and criticized.

For the privileged, there were 1,400 free-standing wooden seats in the Tiger Den, each accompanied by a drink table. There were

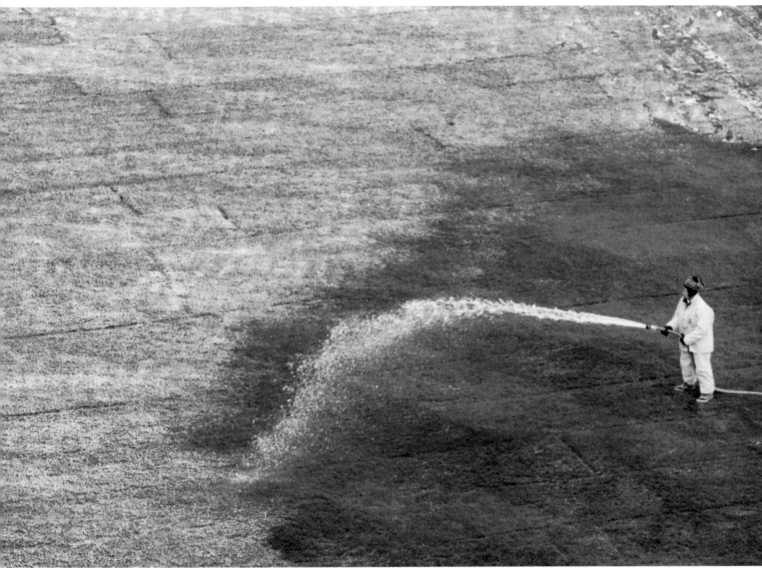

With a splash of water, grounds keeper Gail DeGennaroro turned Snomerica Park's turf into the green grass of home.

102 luxury suites sandwiched between the upper and lower bowls. And there were high-class restaurants and lounges, at your service.

For the not-so-privileged, there were cheaper seats without obstructed views and a small bleacher section with $8 tickets. There were places to buy hot dogs and sausages and beverages.

For the children, there were a Ferris wheel and a carousel, tastefully located where they couldn't be seen from the field and stands. And, of course, there was a souvenir shop, stocked full with good

stuff. *Can I get a Tigers cap, Dad? If you're good, son.*

For the teams, there was ecstasy. The Tigers' clubhouse is so huge that rookies might get lost if they're not careful. So is the training room. And weight room. And video room. And equipment room. And underground batting cage. And lounge. The players have so many places to feel renewed pride.

In the concourse were pictures of every era of Tigers baseball. Out on the brick centerfield wall were the numbers and names of the Tigers' greatest players. Cobb. Greenberg. Gehringer. Newhouser.

Kaline. Cochrane and Crawford and Heilmann and Jennings and Manush. In left-center were stainless steel statues of Detroit's Hall of Famers.

History had not been forgotten.

Still, something wasn't quite right.

"I kind of feel like we're on the road right now," Moehler said.

This was where the Tigers played? So much seemed foreign. Escalators? A centerfield fountain? Posh suites? Strobe lights? Space? The park looked like it belonged to someone else. A bigger market, maybe. A new market, maybe. ➤➤

A fancy-dancy dot-com community, maybe. Not the roll-up-your-sleeves Motor City.

In some ways, it was easy to start missing an old friend, which you knew was now sitting sadly by the side of the road, empty, for the first time since 1912. Hadn't we forgotten something?

Tiger Stadium.

If this was Opening Day, if this was a Tigers game, where were those lovable flaws that connected your experience to your grandfather's? The chipping paint? The sausage smells stained into the walls? The cramped concourses? The intolerable toilets? The long lines? The poles? Where were the dugouts with the low ceilings that left lumps on Lance Parrish's head?

Where were the ghosts of your heroes?

First you were curious. Then you were uncomfortable. *This is nice. Really nice. But not mine.*

Beneath the stands in the new manager's office was the Tigers' new manager, Phil Garner. He sat in his sterile office — no pictures on the wall yet, cardboard boxes together with cigar boxes on the desk — and talked. He joked about the weather. ("Just a warm day in Canada, isn't it?") He talked about Comerica Park. ("It's beautiful out there.") He talked about living nearby in an apartment in the old Stroh's Brewery. ("I wish they still had those vats in there.") He talked about the team. ("We've got to play better.")

All the while, he was getting to know people who were getting to know him. Then, suddenly, a familiar face popped in, and a familiar voice sounded off as if it were coming out of a nearby television set.

"Hello, Mr. Garner," said Tigers Hall of Famer and former broadcaster George Kell, dressed in full uniform for a pregame ceremony.

"You gonna play today?" Gar-

What windchill? Joe (Bubba) Baker of Warren was one of 39,168 hearty patrons who braved the elements.

J. KYLE KEENER

ner asked, smiling and shaking Kell's hand. "Can I get a couple out of you today?"

"Awww," Kell said, "every time I put this thing on, I remember I'm supposed to be wearing a suit."

Everyone laughed. Kell walked out. Garner sat down and resumed talking. But then, in mid-sentence, he stopped, sprang out of his chair, and darted for the door.

"Sparky!" he yelled.

Out in the hallway stood Sparky Anderson. He was in full

uniform, too. When he heard Garner, he turned, smiled and waved him over.

"We need a little help in here with the press," Garner joked.

"Yeah," Sparky said. "Keep feedin' 'em those lines."

And the past blended into the present. Garner didn't seem so foreign. He seemed more like a new friend.

Tiger Stadium didn't seem so far away.

"There's nothing you can misunderstand about Tiger Stadium and its history," slugger Tony Clark said. "As soon as you walk into the stadium, you see all the nooks and crannies, the nicks in the paint, the holes in the walls. A new ballpark doesn't have those. So now it's our opportunity to put our own dents and cuts and scrapes in the walls and everywhere else."

The gates opened and fans spilled into Comerica Park, your friends, your family, your neighbors, the same folks you shared summers with at the corner of Michigan and Trumbull.

Opening Day, although gray and gross, taught Detroit that anything could change. After one afternoon, Comerica Park showed it is the polar opposite of Tiger Stadium. While Tiger Stadium's stacked stands seemed to shelter the city from its ugly image in its later years, Comerica Park's open and airy design seems to invite the city to look at itself again, to like what it sees, to dream boldly of what comes next. And to come back and do it again and again.

For so long, Detroit had grasped the past so tightly that it had crumbled. Finally, Detroit, while remembering its roots, has built something symbolic of something else.

Hope for a new season.
Hope for a new city.
Hope for a new age.
Hope. ◆

DAVID P. GILKEY

Hal Newhouser stood tall in his playing days and does so again.

Comerica Park's design invited fans to look out while allowing pedestrians to look in.

KENT PHILLIPS

POMP AND HAPPENSTANCE

By Brian Murphy

SUSAN TUSA

Mother Nature did more than just sneak a cold, wet curveball past the Tigers, Seattle Mariners and 39,168 people who huddled inside Comerica Park. She also dampened pregame ceremonies for the team's 100th American League home opener with a steady repertoire of snow, sleet and slop.

Festivities were delayed while the grounds crew siphoned slush from the outfield and let the infield breathe without a tarp over it. A flyover by F-16 fighter planes from Selfridge Air National Guard Base in Macomb County was scrapped because of murky skies. So was the drop-in of an Air Force parachutist, who was to deliver the first-pitch ball and the resin bag to the mound.

"We had to implode that," Tigers spokesman Tyler Barnes said.

Despite the circumstances, the Comerica inauguration wasn't without pomp, although it was more reserved than the September 1999 swan song at Tiger Stadium.

Sixty-three former Tigers took part that day, forming a human chain to pass the Tigers' team flag to catcher Brad Ausmus to take to the new park.

For the 2000 opener, the process was reversed, with former Tigers pitcher Eldon Auker (1933-38) sending it along a line of players before it went up the flag-pole in left-centerfield — a location similar to that at Tiger Stadium.

Besides the 89-year-old Auker, Willie Horton, George Kell and Al Kaline also were in uniform. But the largest ovation was saved for the little, white-haired professor who managed the Tigers to more victories (1,331) than anyone else and to their World Series title in 1984.

Sparky Anderson, who retired in 1995 after 17 years with the Tigers, stopped at Comerica Park on his way to Cooperstown and induction into the Baseball Hall of Fame.

The only manager to win World Series in both leagues offered his assessment of the American League's newest park.

"This is fantastic. Just beautiful," Anderson beamed. "Anytime you can see the city's skyline, it's a great stadium."

In acknowledging its past, the team also recognized its future and those who built it.

Maggie Dewald, 9, of Hamtramck; Jack Barthwell, 10, of Detroit; and Alessi Nehr, 9, of Farmington Hills were wandering through the concourse with their parents when team officials asked if they wanted to participate in the ceremonial first pitches.

Within minutes, they were on the field, and Dewald — not the mayor, governor or some other politico — hurled the first Comerica Park strike.

Then there were the men and women who poured the concrete, riveted the girders and laid the mortar that transformed the big hole off Woodward Avenue into Comerica Park. There was still a bit of heavy lifting to do.

More than 260 construction workers carried out and unfolded

the largest American flag in the country for the national anthem — 150-by-300 feet of Old Glory stitched together by the San Diego-based company Wizard of Ahs.

And just like the fans who took in the sparkling ballpark for the first time, the politicians and team officials — from Gov. John Engler and Mayor Dennis Archer to Tigers owner Mike Ilitch and team president John McHale — basked in the chilly afterglow of their campaign to bring the Tigers into the modern era.

"I am delighted to welcome everybody to the city where dreams come true," Archer said. ◆

Despite sloppy conditions, it was a banner day as construction workers who built Comerica Park unfurled a gigantic Old Glory.

PAUL WARNER/Associated Press

Sparky Anderson, who had been elected to the Hall of Fame a few weeks before
the opener, was a hit with future big-leaguers. But the Ferris wheel with cars
shaped like baseballs was a miss, not quite ready for Comerica Park's debut.

SUSAN TUSA

Corner to Copa: The Tigers' team flag that flew over Michigan and Trumbull was hand-delivered to its new home.

J. KYLE KEENER

MORE EXPANSIVE AND EXPENSIVE

Most seats were closer to the playing field at Tiger Stadium than they are at Comerica Park. For instance, the back row of upper deck seats at Tiger Stadium was 160 feet from home plate — the same distance as the first row of upper deck seats at Comerica Park. But the new ballpark has its advantages. Here's a rundown of pluses and minuses of Comerica Park:

Pluses:
➤ No annoying posts or obstructed views
➤ Angled seats
➤ More seats grouped around bases

Minuses:
➤ Seats farther away
➤ More gradual slope in lower deck seats might make it tougher to see over heads of people in front
➤ More exposed to sun and rain

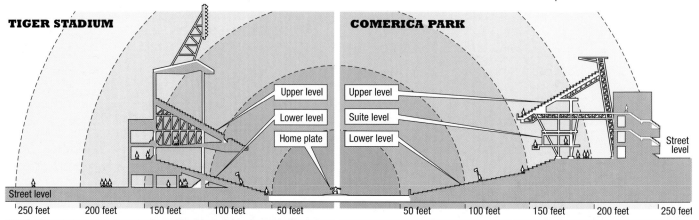

TIGER STADIUM

Upper level
Lower level
Home plate

COMERICA PARK

Upper level
Suite level
Lower level

Street level

Street level

| 250 feet | 200 feet | 150 feet | 100 feet | 50 feet | | 50 feet | 100 feet | 150 feet | 200 feet | 250 feet |

TIGER STADIUM 1999

Tickets to see the Tigers have gone up in price at the new ballpark.

LOWER DECK	SEATS	PRICE	UPPER DECK	SEATS	PRICE
Tiger Den	3,191	$25	Tiger Den	600	$25
Box	3,222	$20	Box	3,343	$20
Reserved	5,131	$15	Box (outfield)	1,372	$15
Reserved (outfield)	5,062	$12	Reserved	5,147	$12
Leftfield grandstand	5,265	$10	Reserved (outfield)	7,958	$8
Rightfield grandstand	955	$8	Bleacher	5,800	$5

COMERICA PARK 2000

LOWER LEVEL (19,000 seats)	PRICE	UPPER LEVEL (11,000 seats)	PRICE	PREMIUM	PRICE
Infield box	$30	Upper box	$20	Tiger Den	$75
Outfield box	$25	Upper box (outfield)	$20	Tiger Den (1,400 Tiger Den seats)	$60
Pavilion	$14	Mezzanine	$15	On-deck circle (1,200 seats)	$60
Fan stands (1,000 seats)	$8	Upper reserved	$12	Club seats (1,400 seats)	$50
				Suites (not shown, 2,000 seats)	$90,000 to $150,000 per season

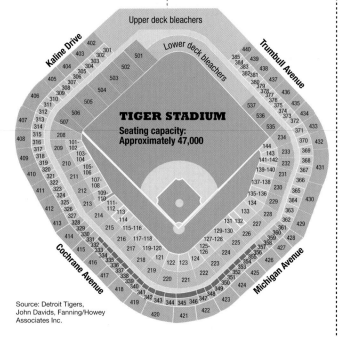

TIGER STADIUM
Seating capacity: Approximately 47,000

Source: Detroit Tigers, John Davids, Fanning/Howey Associates Inc.

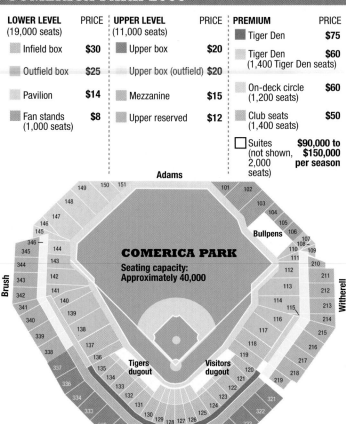

COMERICA PARK
Seating capacity: Approximately 40,000

MARTHA THIERRY/ Detroit Free Press

OUR
HEROES

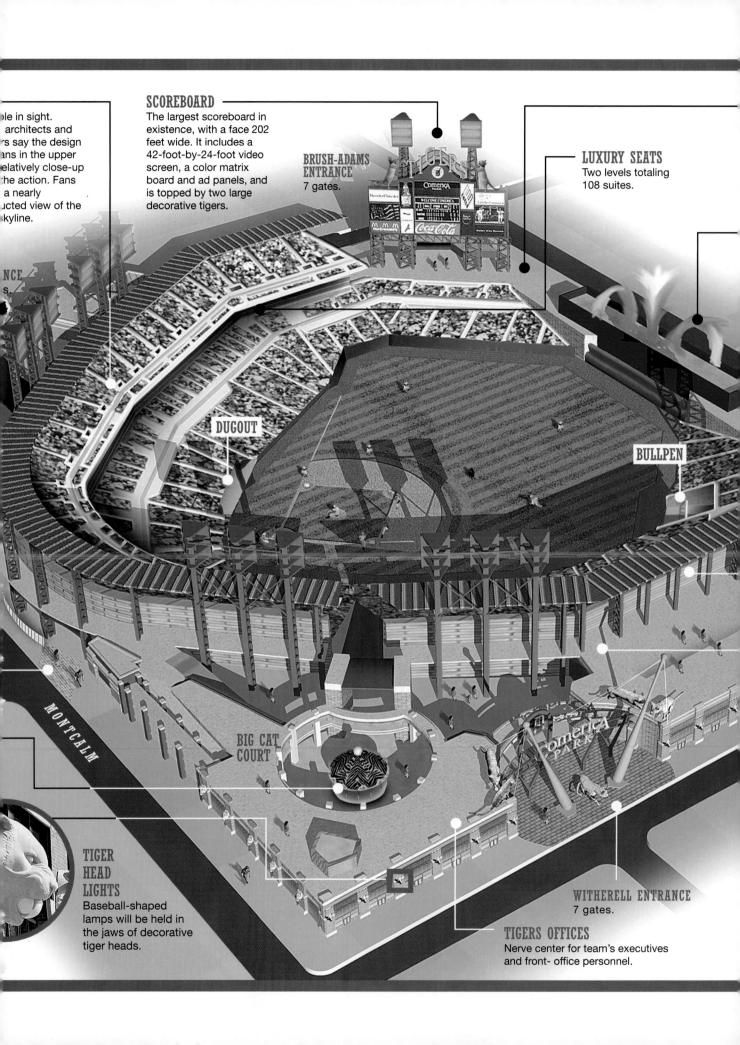

SCOREBOARD
The largest scoreboard in existence, with a face 202 feet wide. It includes a 42-foot-by-24-foot video screen, a color matrix board and ad panels, and is topped by two large decorative tigers.

BRUSH-ADAMS ENTRANCE
7 gates.

LUXURY SEATS
Two levels totaling 108 suites.

...le in sight. ...architects and ...s say the design ...ns in the upper ...elatively close-up ...he action. Fans ...a nearly ...ucted view of the ...kyline.

...NCE ...s.

DUGOUT

BULLPEN

BIG CAT COURT

MONTCALM

TIGER HEAD LIGHTS
Baseball-shaped lamps will be held in the jaws of decorative tiger heads.

WITHERELL ENTRANCE
7 gates.

TIGERS OFFICES
Nerve center for team's executives and front- office personnel.

FERRIS WHEEL
Located near the third base side of the main concourse, the Italian-designed 50-foot-high Fly Ball Ferris wheel features 12 cars shaped like baseballs that can hold five passengers each.

VIEW -
Not a p
Ballpar
enginee
allows
deck a
view of
also ge
unobst
Detroit

DOWNTOWN DETROIT BEER HALL
Features a 70-foot bar and offers a large selection of local and international beers.

BRUSH
ENTRA
2 gat

BRUSHFIRE GRILL
A 16,000-square-foot open-air garden with picnic tables offering barbecued turkey, ribs and beef as well as salmon and veggie burgers. A giant floating baseball will bob in a water fountain.

BRUSH

PARKING GARAGE
About 1,000 parking spaces were added with the construction of a multi-level garage adjacent to the north side of the ballpark.

TIGER'S DEN
A 5,400-square-foot lounge that features free-standing tables, comfortable chairs and 450 lockers in which to store your stuff.

VIP ENTRANCE
The Montcalm entrance features eight gates for club patrons.

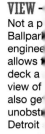

CAROUSEL
The centerpiece of Big Cat Court, located on the first base side of the main concourse. Big Cat carousel offers fans a chance to ride atop 30 handcrafted and painted tigers. Thirty-six feet in diameter, the ride is accessible to wheelchairs and features two chariots.

Spikes high, Ty Cobb slides into third base. Hal Newhouser
kicks and deals. Charlie Gehringer turns a double play.
Al Kaline leaps for a ball. Hank Greenberg tees up an
awesome home run. The five sculptures that grace Comerica
Park rekindle images of Detroit's greatest ballplayers, frozen
in time through the stainless-steel artistry of Pennsylvania
sculptors Omri Amrany and his wife, Julie Rotblatt-Amrany.

HALL OF FAME STATUES

A series of statues located along the left-centerfield wall celebrates five Tigers Hall of Famers. Cast in stainless steel are Ty Cobb, Charlie Gehringer, Hank Greenberg, Hal Newhouser and Al Kaline. Each is about 13 feet high.

LIQUID FIREWORKS

The centerfield wall features a fountain that will produce a liquid fireworks display programmed to music and light changes. Will celebrate home runs and other in-game events. Water can spray 150 feet in the air.

PITCH INFORMATION

For the baseball aficionado, a board displaying the type of pitch thrown as well as the speed of the pitch.

TIGER CLUB

A 20,000-square-foot membership club with more than 400 seats. Overlooks rightfield and offers field views through its glass walls. Features three bars and a dining buffet as well as a cigar lounge.

THE SEATS

Fixed seats at Comerica Park are dark green and horizontally slat-backed, similar to seats in older ballparks. Made of sturdy plastic, they are designed and manufactured by American Seating of Grand Rapids, which made the seats for old Navin Field. Most fixed seats are 19 inches wide and include a cup holder. All seats are angled to face home plate. Premium seats are 22 inches wide and padded.

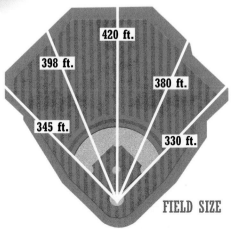

ADAMS

WITHERELL

GRAND CIRCUS ENTRANCE
13 gates.

CONCOURSES

One of the biggest differences from Tiger Stadium. Concourses are open and airy as well as much wider. They allow for easier passage and for views to the outside of the park as well as the field of play.

FIELD SIZE

420 ft.
398 ft.
380 ft.
345 ft.
330 ft.

LOCATION

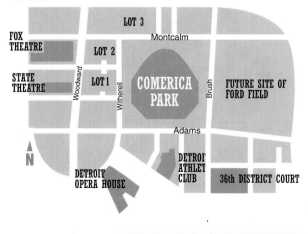

FOX THEATRE
STATE THEATRE
LOT 3
LOT 2
LOT 1
Montcalm
Woodward
Witherell
COMERICA PARK
Brush
Adams
FUTURE SITE OF FORD FIELD
N
DETROIT OPERA HOUSE
DETROIT ATHLETIC CLUB
36th DISTRICT COURT

CREDITS:
ART: Rick Nease
PHOTOS: Kent Phillips, J. Kyle Keener, Tom Pidgeon
TEXT: David A. Markiewicz

Brian Moehler delivered Comerica Park's first pitch — a strike — at 1:18 p.m. Tuesday, April 11, 2000.

J. KYLE KEENER

TIGERS ARE IN GOOD HANDS

By John Lowe

All sorts of things happened in the first game at spacious Comerica Park that seldom or never would have happened at cozy Tiger Stadium.

Tigers catcher Brad Ausmus repeatedly called for pitches down the middle, inviting hitters to hit the ball toward the distant fences. Seattle never came close to hitting a home run, stranding runners galore in scoring position as Brian Moehler and his bullpen collected a 5-2 victory before a capacity crowd of 39,168.

The Tigers parlayed walks and triples into two-run rallies in the first and second innings. They did something they did only five times the past two seasons at Tiger Stadium — win without a home run.

But one thing that never would have happened at Tiger Stadium had nothing to do with the change in ballparks. It had to do with 20 pounds that Tigers first baseman Tony Clark lost over the winter, making him faster on the bases and more agile on defense.

With none out in the sixth inning, with Moehler losing his ➤➤

stuff and with the tying run on base, Clark dove to his right to rob Mark McLemore of the hit that could have turned the game around. Clark bounded up and tagged retreating Carlos Guillen for a rally-killing, unassisted double play. Both managers called it the game's key play.

"There's an unbelievable amount of satisfaction to know that defensively you're not a liability," Clark said. "All the hard work, sweat and time that you put together in the off-season comes to a head on a play like today."

"If that ball gets through," McLemore said, "I'd think he

(Moehler) was in trouble. There's probably a run in and runners on second and third. But Clark made a nice play."

From Nov. 1 until mid-February, Clark stuck to this regimen to lose weight: running on a treadmill for two hours a day twice a week; riding a bike for 45 minutes five or six times a week; and lifting weights for two hours a day four times a week.

You never know when it'll pay off. But it did in the sixth inning.

After trailing, 4-0, Seattle scored in the fourth and fifth innings. The fifth-inning run was the big-league-high 13th unearned run allowed by

the Tigers in their seven-game season, and the fourth traceable to an error by Juan Encarnacion.

Encarnacion, the centerfielder, became the first Tiger booed at Comerica Park when he let Jay Buhner's two-out single skip past him, allowing John Olerud to score from first. It was Encarnacion's third error this season.

Dan Wilson opened the sixth with a rare infield single by a catcher, a slow roller toward third. Guillen, the No. 9 hitter, fouled two 2-2 pitches before drawing Moehler's first walk.

It was first and second with none out, and danger loomed. ➤➤

MOEHLER HITS THE SPOT

Emotionally, the opener at Comerica Park was something special for the man who would throw the first pitch. Strategy-wise, though, it was business as usual for Tigers starter Brian Moehler. So while getting a grip on his nerves wasn't easy, his choice of what to throw to Seattle Mariners leadoff hitter Mark McLemore was.

"Every start, you look fastball first pitch," Moehler said after notching the first "W" at Comerica Park. "You throw a fastball right down the middle and let them hit the ball. If they hit it out, they hit it out."

Moehler said the strategy held true "especially in this park," which he and other Tigers agreed was a pitcher's best friend. And the fact that McLemore was Seattle manager Lou Piniella's leadoff batter made Moehler's first-pitch choice simpler, he said.

"Most guys aren't going to swing at the first pitch leading off," Moehler said. "Occasionally you'll get a guy, especially a rookie or a first-year guy playing in a new ballpark, and he'll say I'm going to try and hit this ball out. Make a statement.

"McLemore's a veteran. He's trying to get on base."

And, in fact, McLemore took that first-pitch fastball, which Moehler drilled over the heart of the plate for a strike. It was a positive omen for what would be a strong six-inning outing. Not that Moehler had any doubts beforehand. Just jitters.

"I was a little juiced up," he said, "and I talked to our sports psychologist. I have a tendency to get a little worked up and overthrow.

"Anytime you pitch a game like this," Moehler said, "a home opener of this magnitude, there's

Before making first-pitch history, Tigers starter Brian Moehler confessed, "I was a little juiced up."

KIRTHMON F. DOZIER

going to be some butterflies and nerves. I was just trying to get the first inning over with. I wasn't trying to overthrow.

"Just hit my spots."

Moehler hit his spot, and the ball wound up in the Baseball Hall of Fame in Cooperstown, N.Y.◆
– By David A. Markiewicz

JULIAN H. GONZALEZ

A RESOUNDING HIT, SORT OF

John Olerud stood on second base in the first inning and thought for a moment. He had just slapped a double, the first hit at Comerica Park. Tears streamed down his face, and the next thing he knew, he was overcome with emotion and he knelt on one knee and cried.

Really?

No, not really. Oh, Olerud (connecting, above) did realize he had just done something historic.

"The thought crossed my mind," said Olerud, Seattle's first baseman. "Probably the biggest thing is I'll be the answer to a trivia question. I'll be able to tell my kids, that sort of thing.

"Whether they'll be impressed by that, I don't know." ◆
— *By Michael Rosenberg*

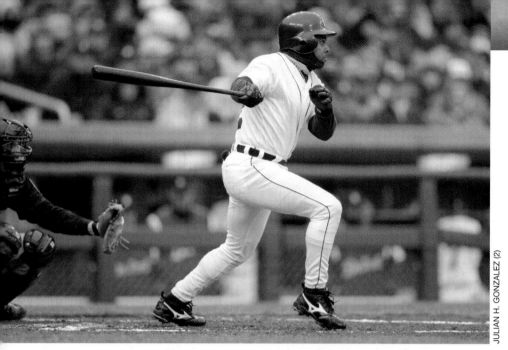

JULIAN H. GONZALEZ (2)

Luis Polonia got the Tigers going with a leadoff triple, and first baseman Tony Clark saved the day by turning an unassisted double play.

Moehler knew he was losing steam, it was too early for the bullpen to guard the lead, and the top of the order was up.

McLemore, who had flied to Encarnacion on the first at-bat in Comerica history, made better contact when he rifled an 0-1 pitch toward the rightfield corner. The 6-foot-7 Clark went from upright to horizontal in a flash, like the arm on a traffic gate suddenly closing. Clark was on the grass guarding against a bunt — giving him less time to react and making the catch more impressive.

As suddenly as he made the catch, Clark sprang up and scampered for the bag, tagging Guillen as he slid. Double play. Moehler got Mike Cameron on a fly ball, preventing Alex Rodriguez from batting in the inning as the potential tying run. In the split second between the time the ball left McLemore's bat and entered Clark's glove, it seemed certain that Rodriguez would get his 42-homer bat to the plate in the sixth.

Clark's catch culminated six innings of offensive frustration by the Mariners and escape artistry by Moehler. When the top of the sixth ended, the Mariners were outhit-

ting the Tigers, 10-5, but were 2-for-12 with runners in scoring position, stranding seven runners on second or third.

In contrast to their 1-5 season-opening trip, the Tigers got the hits they needed with runners in scoring position. Before they made an out in their new home, they had scored on Luis Polonia's triple and Gregg Jefferies' single.

Then walks became important. With two out in the first, Ausmus and Dean Palmer walked against right-hander Freddy Garcia, pushing Jefferies to third. When Garcia made a false start in his windup while pitching to Karim Garcia, it wasn't just a balk — it was a run-scoring balk and a 2-0 lead.

Encarnacion singled to begin the second, and Deivi Cruz used the first of his three sacrifice bunts, sending him to second. Polonia, who walked about once a week in 1999, rallied from 0-2 for a walk. One out later, Bobby Higginson did something he didn't do in '99 — hit a triple. In Tiger Stadium, with its shorter power gaps, the same ball likely would have been a double.

Encarnacion, who walked less than once a week in '99, walked to

start the sixth and scored on Cruz's next sacrifice and Jefferies' single. The Tigers had scored five off Garcia — matching their total in three losses to him in 1999.

That's how to win without a homer. "You might see a number of those this year," Ausmus said.

"We can win without hitting the ball out," Polonia said. "Even the heavy guys are going to hit triples."

That might include Clark, given that he weighs 233 — the weight he has maintained since the start of training camp.

You won't read anything about Clark in the offensive summary. He fanned during the two-run first and grounded out to end the two-run second. That made him 4-for-21 in 2000. Yet this slow-hitting start hasn't detracted from his defense — perhaps adding to it.

On a day when everyone needed mittens, Comerica Park fit the Tigers like a glove — a first baseman's glove. ◆

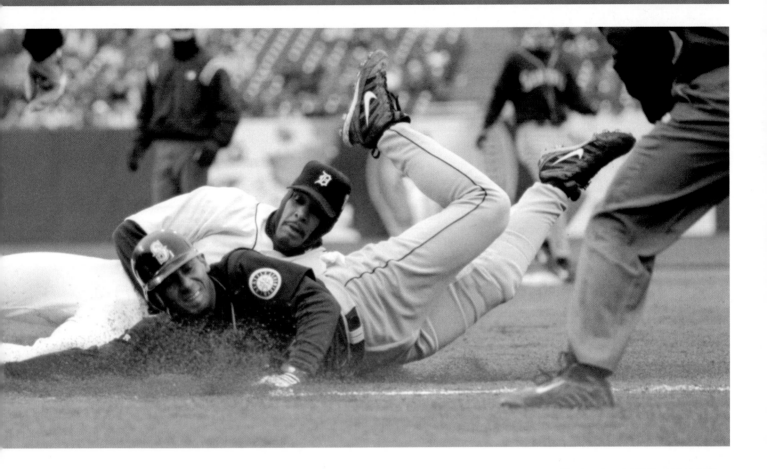

THE FIRST CALLS FROM COMERICA PARK

ERNIE HARWELL,
right, WJR-AM (760):

"Well, here we go. McLemore will
lead it off. Here's the first pitch at
Comerica — and it's a strike
called. I talked to Mac before the
game. I said, 'Ever done anything
like that before?' He said, 'No,
but I'm ready.' "

JOSH LEWIN,
Fox Sports Net:

"Anticipation gives way to reality
right here. Strike one called by a
native Detroiter, Rick Reed,
behind the plate. Reed, by the
way, switched with a couple of
other umpires to make sure he
could be here today. A guy that
grew up in the Six Mile and Gra-
tiot area. He and his friends used
to sneak into Tiger Stadium."

TIGERS LINEUP

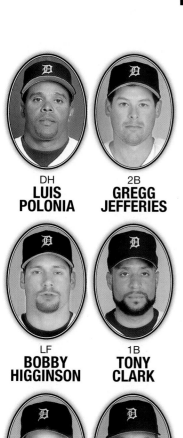

DH
LUIS POLONIA

2B
GREGG JEFFERIES

LF
BOBBY HIGGINSON

1B
TONY CLARK

C
BRAD AUSMUS

3B
DEAN PALMER

RF
KARIM GARCIA

CF
JUAN ENCARNACION

SS
DEIVI CRUZ

P
BRIAN MOEHLER

SEATTLE	ab	r	h	rbi	bb	so	avg.
McLemore lf-2b	5	0	0	0	0	0	.174
Cameron cf	4	0	0	0	1	1	.207
Rodriguez ss	4	0	2	0	1	1	.333
Olerud 1b	5	1	3	0	0	0	.261
Martinez dh	5	0	0	0	0	2	.167
Buhner rf	5	0	3	0	0	0	.435
Bell 2b	3	0	0	0	0	0	.136
a-Mabry ph-lf	1	0	0	0	0	1	.100
Wilson c	4	1	3	0	0	0	.250
Guillen 3b	3	0	1	1	1	1	.091
Totals	39	2	12	1	3	6	

DETROIT	ab	r	h	rbi	bb	so	avg.
Polonia dh	4	2	1	0	1	0	.130
Jefferies 2b	4	1	2	2	0	1	.375
Halter 2b	1	0	0	0	0	0	.167
Higginson lf	4	0	1	2	0	0	.214
Clark 1b	4	0	1	0	0	1	.217
Ausmus c	3	0	0	0	1	0	.400
Palmer 3b	2	0	0	0	2	1	.231
Garcia rf	4	0	0	0	0	3	.000
Encarnacion cf	3	2	2	0	1	0	.346
Cruz ss	1	0	1	0	0	0	.333
Totals	30	5	8	4	5	6	

SEATTLE				000	110	000	–	2	12	2
DETROIT				220	001	00x	–	5	8	3

a-struck out for Bell in the 7th.
E: Cameron (1), Wilson (1), Palmer (3), Encarnacion (3), Cruz (1). **LOB:** Seattle 13, Detroit 9. **2B:** Olerud (1), Wilson (1), Guillen (1), Encarnacion (1), Cruz (3). **3B:** Polonia (2), Higginson (1). **RBI:** Guillen (1), Jefferies (2), Higginson 2 (2). **S:** Cruz (3).
Runners left in scoring position: Seattle 9 (McLemore, Cameron 2, Martinez 2, Buhner 2, Bell, Mabry. Detroit 6 (Halter, Higginson 2, Clark, Garcia 2). **Runners moved up:** McLemore, Bell, Jefferies.
DP: Detroit 1 (Clark).

SEATTLE	ip	h	r	er	bb	so	np	avg.
Garcia (L 1-1)	6	6	5	5	5	4	118	5.73
Paniagua	2	2	0	0	0	2	23	0.00

DETROIT	ip	h	r	er	bb	so	np	avg.
Moehler (W 1-1)	6	10	2	1	1	3	107	3.00
Patterson	2/3	1	0	0	1	0	16	0.00
Brocail	1 1/3	0	0	0	0	1	19	5.79
Jones (S 2)	1	1	0	0	1	2	23	0.00

Inherited runners-scored: Brocail 2-0.
Balk: (Garcia) 1.
T: 3:12. **A:** 39,168.
Umpires: Home, Reed; 1b, Wegner; 2b, Reynolds; 3b, Williams.

PLAY-BY-PLAY

FIRST INNING

MARINERS: McLemore flied to centerfielder Encarnacion. Cameron safe on Cruz's error. Cameron was picked off, pitcher Moehler to first baseman Clark. Rodriguez safe on Palmer's error. Olerud doubled to right, Rodriguez to third. Martinez flied to right-fielder Garcia. 0 runs, 1 hit, 2 errors, 2 left on. **Tigers 0, Mariners 0.**

TIGERS: Polonia tripled to center. Jefferies singled to right, Polonia scored. Higginson flied to centerfielder Cameron. Clark struck out. Ausmus walked on a full count, Jefferies to second. Palmer walked on a full count, Jefferies to third, Ausmus to second. On Garcia's balk, Jefferies scored, Ausmus to third, Palmer to second. Garcia struck out. 2 runs, 2 hits, 0 errors, 2 left on. **Tigers 2, Mariners 0.**

SECOND INNING

MARINERS: Buhner infield single to second. Bell grounded out, shortstop Cruz to first baseman Clark, Buhner to second. Wilson singled to left, Buhner to third. Guillen struck out. McLemore flied to centerfielder Encarnacion. 0 runs, 2 hits, 0 errors, 2 left on. **Tigers 2, Mariners 0.**

TIGERS: Encarnacion singled to left. Cruz sacrificed, first baseman Olerud to second baseman Bell, Encarnacion to second. Polonia walked on a full count. Jefferies struck out. Higginson tripled to center, Encarnacion and Polonia scored. Clark grounded out, second baseman Bell to first baseman Olerud. 2 runs, 2 hits, 0 errors, 1 left on. Tigers 4, Mariners 0.

THIRD INNING

MARINERS: Cameron popped to shortstop Cruz. Rodriguez singled to left. Olerud singled to left, Rodriguez to third. Martinez struck out. Buhner grounded into fielder's choice, third baseman Palmer to second baseman Jefferies, Olerud out. 0 runs, 2 hits, 0 errors, 2 left on. Tigers 4, Mariners 0.

TIGERS: Ausmus grounded out, third baseman Guillen to first baseman Olerud. Palmer safe on Wilson's error. Garcia fouled to third baseman Guillen. Encarnacion grounded out, shortstop Rodriguez to first baseman Olerud. 0 runs, 0 hits, 1 error, 1 left on. Tigers 4, Mariners 0.

FOURTH INNING

MARINERS: Bell grounded out, first baseman Clark to pitcher Moehler. Wilson doubled to right. Guillen doubled to right, Wilson scored. McLemore grounded out, second baseman Jefferies to first baseman Clark, Guillen to third. Cameron struck out. 1 run, 2 hits, 0 errors, 1 left on. Tigers 4, Mariners 1.

TIGERS: Cruz doubled to center. Polonia popped to third baseman Guillen. Jefferies grounded out, second baseman Bell to first baseman Olerud, Cruz to third. Higginson flied to centerfielder Cameron. 0 runs, 1 hit, 0 errors, 1 left on. Tigers 4, Mariners 1.

FIFTH INNING

MARINERS: Rodriguez singled to center. Olerud grounded into fielder's choice, third baseman Palmer to second baseman Jefferies, Rodriguez out. Martinez lined to leftfielder Higginson. Buhner singled to center, Olerud to third. On Encarnacion's error, Olerud scored, Buhner to third. Bell grounded out, pitcher Moehler to first baseman Clark. **1 run, 2 hits, 1 error, 1 left on. Tigers 4, Mariners 2.**

TIGERS: Clark fouled to second baseman Bell. Ausmus grounded out, third baseman Guillen to first baseman Olerud. Palmer walked on a full count. Garcia struck out. **0 runs, 0 hits, 0 errors, 1 left on. Tigers 4, Mariners 2.**

SIXTH INNING

MARINERS: Wilson infield single to third. Guillen walked on a full count, Wilson to second. McLemore lined into a double play, first baseman Clark unassisted, Guillen out. Cameron flied to rightfielder Garcia. **0 runs, 1 hit, 0 errors, 1 left on. Tigers 4, Mariners 2.**

TIGERS: Encarnacion walked. Cruz sacrificed, first baseman Olerud to second baseman Bell, Encarnacion to second. Polonia flied to centerfielder Cameron. Jefferies singled to center, Encarnacion scored. On Cameron's error, Jefferies to second. Higginson grounded out, third baseman Guillen to first baseman Olerud. **1 run, 1 hit, 1 error, 1 left on. Tigers 5, Mariners 2.**

SEVENTH INNING

MARINERS: Patterson pitching. Halter in as second baseman. Rodriguez walked on a full count. Olerud lined to leftfielder Higginson. Martinez flied to rightfielder Garcia. Buhner singled to left, Rodriguez to third. Mabry pinch-hitting for Bell. Brocail pitching. Mabry struck out. **0 runs, 1 hit, 0 errors, 2 left on. Tigers 5, Mariners 2.**

TIGERS: McLemore in as second baseman. Mabry in as leftfielder. Paniagua pitching. Clark singled to right. Ausmus lined to first baseman Olerud. Palmer struck out. Garcia struck out. **0 runs, 1 hit, 0 errors, 1 left on. Tigers 5, Mariners 2.**

EIGHTH INNING

MARINERS: Wilson flied to rightfielder Garcia. Guillen flied to centerfielder Encarnacion. McLemore grounded out, first baseman Clark to pitcher Brocail. **0 runs, 0 hits, 0 errors, 0 left on. Tigers 5, Mariners 2.**

TIGERS: Encarnacion doubled to left. Cruz sacrificed, third baseman Guillen to second baseman McLemore, Encarnacion to third. Polonia flied to leftfielder Mabry. Halter flied to centerfielder Cameron. **0 runs, 1 hit, 0 errors, 1 left on. Tigers 5, Mariners 2.**

JULIAN H. GONZALEZ

NINTH INNING

MARINERS: Jones pitching. Cameron walked on a full count. Rodriguez struck out. Olerud infield single to third, Cameron to second. Martinez struck out. Buhner grounded out, second baseman Halter to first baseman Clark. **0 runs, 1 hit, 0 errors, 2 left on. Tigers 5, Mariners 2.**

Todd Jones, who closed out the Royals in the Tiger Stadium finale, finished off the Mariners in the Comerica Park opener.

KEEPSAKE SCORECARDS

Ernie Harwell, the Tigers Hall of Fame broadcaster, began keeping score at The Corner in 1954, the year he called his first game there. He turned 82 in January 2000 but hasn't missed a beat, and on Opening Day he personally christened Comerica Park when Karim Garcia struck out, ending the first inning: "He stood there like the house by the side of the road and watched that one go by." The Free Press asked Ernie for a glimpse of his scorecards from the last game at Tiger Stadium and the first at Comerica Park, and he happily obliged.

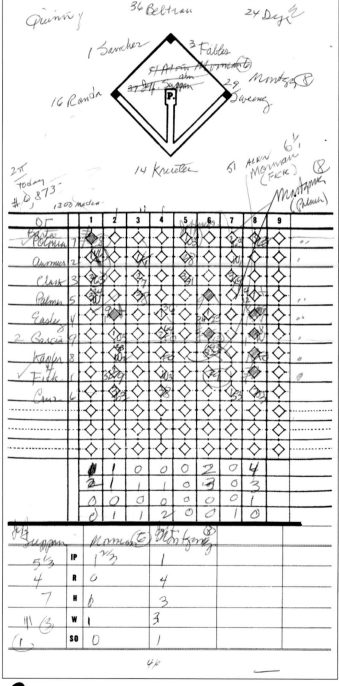

Opening Day at Comerica Park

FUNNIEST SIGN:

THE HOUSE THAT PIZZA BUILT

Historic Firsts at Comerica

FIRST PITCH

FIRST HIT

FIRST DETROIT SPORTS VENUE WITH ADEQUATE RESTROOMS

NO WAITING?

IT'S A MIRACLE

HEEEY! I THOUGHT THEY PROMISED NO TALL POLES BLOCKING THE VIEW...

KISS ME I'M POLISH

THE PARKING SHORTAGE IS WORSE THAN I THOUGHT

TOLEDO CITY LIMITS

COMERICA PARKING $3.00

SUSAN TUSA

FOR FANS, IT WAS LOVE AT FIRST SIGHT

By Tina Lam

After 104 years, baseball in Detroit had a new home. Fans welcomed it with a sense of awe but also as if it already were an old friend. They took pictures of each other in front of the huge tiger at the main entrance to Comerica Park. They reverently touched the larger-than-life-size statues of Ty Cobb, Hank Greenberg, Charlie Gehringer, Hal Newhouser and Al Kaline. They giggled as children and adults rode the carousel. They got used to new seats, new parking places, a new view of the city's skyline, and newly busy streets in an area usually dead quiet on a Tuesday afternoon.

As sometimes happens with an old friend, there were irritations, too. Long lines formed for everything from hot dogs to bathrooms. An escalator didn't work. And some shops and ➤➤

restaurants hadn't opened.

And it was just plain cold — with temperatures hovering around 34 degrees and windchills in the low 20s.

Despite it all, even some fans who expected not to like Comerica Park were won over. The word used most often was awesome.

"I'm more impressed than I thought I would be," said Brett Broich of Ann Arbor. "A lot of articles and messages on the Tigers' Web site said it wasn't great and you'd be far away from the action. I love it."

Broich, sitting in the grandstand in far rightfield instead of his old bleacher seats at Tiger Stadium, said the new view was better.

Cullen Barrie expected the carousel, Ferris wheel and decorating touches to make it feel like an amusement park. "I said that's dumb, that's not baseball," said

Holy Toledo Mud Hens, Batman, fans like Matthew Flaker (below) were willing to do almost anything for ducats.

Barrie, who grew up in Adrian. "When I got here, I liked the carousel. I wanted to ride it.

"If people could have seen the finished Comerica Park when Tiger Stadium closed, I don't think they'd have been so upset. You feel like you're part of downtown Detroit."

Downtown buzzed with activity, from People Mover cars that were jammed by 10:30 a.m. — 2½ hours before game time — to people walking on sidewalks that usually would be empty. Comerica Park was intended to spur development of restaurants and bars in the area, bringing life and people to the city's core.

Most fans said they had little trouble finding parking. What they had the most trouble with was long lines, one of the things the Tigers had promised to fix in a new stadium. Some people gave up trying to buy hot dogs and beer after ⟩⟩

KENT PHILLIPS (2)

CORNER TO COPA

When the Tigers would win a few, then lose a few, George Kell would say they were on a roller-coaster ride. At Comerica Park, fans took merry-go-round rides on Opening Day.

J. KYLE KEENER (2)

Ground rules: The men's-room lines were as long as the beer lines, and vice versa.

standing in lines that moved slowly.

Glitches were evident even in the more luxurious parts of the stadium.

James Moore was annoyed after waiting 20 minutes in line to join three friends inside the exclusive Tiger Club. "This is very disappointing," he said. "You expect if you buy the seats, you'll get to use the privileges."

The stadium also had promised to be family-friendly, and people with children were happy with what they found.

"My first impression of this place is that it's more family-oriented than Tiger Stadium," said Jeff Brower of Trenton. He and friend Greg Bliznik brought their

6-year-old sons, Ryan Brower and Alexander Bliznik, to the home opener. The boys rode the carousel and proclaimed it a good ride.

In the plaza behind rightfield, 7-year-old Lauren Haight of Waterford danced a spontaneous jig late in the game, chanting: "This is great!" Lauren and her father, Todd Haight, also attended the last game at Tiger Stadium. What did she like so much about Comerica Park? "The kid rides," she said. "And there's all kinds of tigers, orange ones and white ones."

Maybe Ernie Harwell said it best in his pregame remarks: "Comerica redefines what a day at the ballpark means." ◆

KETCHUP, TIGERS … KETCHUP!

The crowd was disgusted — screaming and jeering — over hot dogs.

"I'll give you $15 for three of them!" a woman yelled.

But the three workers behind the counter couldn't do anything. They couldn't cook the hot dogs fast enough and their cash register wouldn't work, so they had to make change by hand.

Ron Brierley was finally at the front of the line, after waiting for an hour.

"I've been here since the first pitch," Brierley said. "It's supply and demand. I'm waiting because I'm hungry."

Brierley planned to order 10 hot dogs for his friends. His friend Ellis Bates was waiting in the beer line. A few minutes later, Bates showed up empty-handed. "They ran out of beer," he said. "I waited 45 minutes."

That was the case throughout Comerica Park, as fans waited in long lines for food and beer, especially on the main concourse. The lines were shorter, at times, in the upper deck.

Throughout the stadium, several booths ran out of beer by the second inning.

After Brierley finally got his hot dogs, he turned to the condiment station.

"There's no ketchup," he sighed. "I can't believe this."

There were long lines for beer and hot dogs, but six workers looked almost bored standing behind the counter at the Big Chill, which serves flavored ice and frozen candy.

"We're just chillin' today," said manager Janet Williams. ◆

– By Jeff Seidel

KIRTHMON F. DOZIER

Food lines were long, but for Ian Waller (opposite page) it was mission accomplished.

CORKTOWN: SHUTTLE DIPLOMACY

For one eerie moment, it seemed as if the voice was coming from Tiger Stadium: "Don't bring me down, don't bring me down."

Turns out the words were really "Don't *let* me down," bouncing off Tiger Stadium's aluminum skin from the band playing outside Hoot Robinson's.

Except for the absence of baseball at The Corner, the new facade on the Designated Hatter souvenir shop and scores of shuttle buses tearing down Michigan Avenue, it was bustling business as usual at Corktown's oases.

Sure, Michigan and Trumbull without baseball for the first time in more than 100 years was hardly a minor difference, but hundreds, if not thousands, of fans still jammed Hoot's, Nemo's, Shelley's Place and Reedy's Saloon.

"If you're a fan, you've got to come out!" Dave Sears shouted over the band behind Hoot Robinson's. "They might be playing over there, but the heart's still here — and they know it."

"The crowd's a little thinner," Jennifer Cardella said as she quaffed a pregame libation at Nemo's. "The spirit's still there."

At Reedy's Saloon, owner Tammy Steelman was pleasantly surprised to see a good crowd before the game.

She attributed the turnout to tradition, cheap beer and good food.

Jay Shifman, a longtime Reedy's patron, stayed with his companions to watch the game. He said it was the first time in 27 years he didn't have tickets for Opening Day, blaming the Tigers for saving all but a few hundred tickets for people with season ticket plans.

"There's too much rigmarole to go through," he said. "They were laying bait out there for you. You had to buy 20 tickets."

Although his companions said they preferred Corktown to Foxtown, they predicted bleak days for Detroit's oldest neighborhood.

Tom Cieslinski, drinking a beer under the tent behind Nemo's, agreed that Corktown will eventually lose its traditional business to the area around Comerica Park.

"Maybe next year or this year, people will figure out where to park there," he said.

But at Shelley's Place, celebrating its 48th year of business, owner Shelley Paros said the shuttle buses leaving her place every five minutes would keep the customers coming back.

"Tiger fans are huge traditionalists," she said.

"I don't think anyone will forget about Corktown because this is where it started. ... It's kind of like an institution." ◆
— By M.L. Elrick

NO NORM, NO RON, NO CASH!

All right, so they ran out of beer. And the lines were long. But one thing should have been a lock when Comerica Park opened. Surely the ATMs would work.

Nope.

An hour before the game, one of the three automated teller machines on the main concourse was out of order. Serviceman Al Wallent was called.

"I think it's an electrical problem," he said. "It probably got wet with all of the rain."

As he worked on the machine, people stood in line behind him.

"If we get this thing up and running, maybe I'll go take a look at the game," he said. "I'll probably watch a little, but don't tell my boss." ◆
— By Jeff Seidel

GABRIEL B. TAIT

Ah, the suite life. Here's the view from one of the 102 luxury suites that are sandwiched between the upper and lower bowls.

Les Grey of Farmington Hills found himself in a faraway perch, in the last row in rightfield, but didn't mind:
"The height doesn't bother me," he said. "The stadium architecture
is kind of interesting and reminds me a little of Gotham City in the old Batman movies."

THERE WASN'T A DRY SEAT IN THE HOUSE

When Rick Rojow found his seats along the first baseline, by the visitors dugout, they were sopping wet. And there wasn't an usher in sight.

So he yelled at someone in the dugout.

"Hey, coach!" Rojow yelled. "Throw me a towel to clean my seats!"

The Seattle Mariners coach threw up his arms, like he didn't have one. Then he looked around, found one and tossed it to Rojow.

Rojow, whose family has had Tigers season tickets for about 60 years, was shocked, but he quickly became one of the most popular fans along the first baseline as people asked to borrow his towel to wipe their seats.

He never saw an usher. "I think they are all gone because it's cold," Rojow said.

That was just one of many glitches as workers scrambled to keep fans happy. For example, keeping booths stocked with programs was a challenge as fans were eager to shell out $12 each for the keepsakes.

"They brought 16 of us to help with the programs," said Nelson Pageau, who has sold programs at Tigers games since 1948.

"I think they were probably a dime back in '48," Pageau said. ◆
– By Jeff Seidel

Comerica Park's giant scoreboard — baseball's largest — got mixed reviews from fans. Some praised it for the clarity of the 25-by-42-foot TV screen, but most complained about the number of ads and replays.

"They shouldn't call it a scoreboard — they should call it a billboard," said Josh Carpenter of Milford. "Look at all those ads! The

PICTURE PERFECT, BUT NOT THE ADS

only reason the scoreboard's that big is to accommodate all the ads."

Jason Tremblay of Windsor said they should have put fewer ads on the 202-by-147-foot scoreboard and made the replay screen larger.

He said he would have liked

more replays and hoped the team would use the two other screens for scores from other games and statistics.

Marsha Moore of Novi liked the large screen, the two tigers atop the scoreboard and the old-fashioned look.

"It's a great picture," she said. "That's as clear as my set at home." ◆
– By Dan Shine

WHAT IT COST ON OPENING DAY 2000

**Fans looking for red hots and beer were thrown a curve
— pastries shaped like baseballs.**

J. KYLE KEENER

Cocoa	$1
Coffee	$1
Juice box	$1
Fritos	$1.50
Ice cream sandwich	$1.50
Lil' dog	$1.50
Potato chips	$1.50
Frozen candy bar	$1.75
Candy bar	$2
Cappuccino	$2
Drumstick	$2
Regular popcorn	$2
Small pop	$2
Twizzler	$2
Cracker Jack	$2.25
Malt cup	$2.50
Bottled water	$2.75
Handmade pretzel	$2.75
Hot dog	$2.75
Medium pop	$2.75
Ocean Spray juice	$2.75
Steamed hot dogs	$2.75
Bottled pop	$3
Coney dog	$3
Corn dog	$3
Chicken fingers	$3.25
Large popcorn	$3.25
Chicago-style hot dog	$3.50
Dove bar	$3.50
Fried elephant ears	$3.50
Peanuts	$3.50
Kielbasa	$3.75
Large pop	$3.75
Smoked sausage	$3.75
Nachos	$4
Italian sausage	$4.25
Small beer	$4.50
Medium beer	$5.75
Caesar salad with chicken	$6
Cajun-style catfish sandwich	$6
Chicken sandwich	$6
Corned beef on rye	$6
Hoagie	$6
Italian sub	$6
Jose Cuervo	$6
Nachos grande	$6
Smoked beef with provolone	$6
Turkey sandwich	$6
Gyro in pita	$6.25
Canned beer	$6.75
Large beer	$7.25

J. KYLE KEENER

**Father and son, Joseph and Dennis Toth, braved the elements
for a heartwarming view from behind home plate.**

SEPTEMBER 28, 1999 | COMMEMORATIVE SECTION

TIGER STADIUM
1896 THE CORNER 1999
DETROIT FREE PRESS

TIGERS
ALL-TIME
TEAM
VOTED BY FANS

OF: TY COBB
1905-1926

OF: AL KALINE
1953-1974

OF: KIRK GIBSON
1979-1987
1993-1995

1B: HANK
GREENBERG
1933-1946

2B: CHARLIE
GEHRINGER
1924-1942

3B: GEORGE KELL
1946-1952

SS: ALAN
TRAMMELL
1977-1996

C: BILL FREEHAN
1963-1976

RHP: JACK MORRIS
1977-1990

FINAL GAME	1	2	3	4	5	6	7	8	9	R	H	E
KANSAS CITY	0	1	1	0	0	0	0	0	0	2	11	1
DETROIT	1	1	0	0	0	2	0	4	x	8	11	0

In the gloaming after Monday's game, grounds crew member Charlie McGee digs up home plate.

Out of the park

Fick's slam caps Tigers' 3-HR finale at stadium

By JOHN LOWE
FREE PRESS SPORTS WRITER

Tiger Stadium will be remembered above all for power hitting. That can be true whether you saw hundreds of games there — or only Monday's finale.

Luis Polonia, the 5-foot-8 outfielder, led off the Tigers' first with a stunning, monstrous homer to right-center. Then, with the score tied in the sixth, Karim Garcia lofted an opposite-field drive a few rows into the upper deck in left to put the Tigers in front for good.

And then . . . and then . . . oh, my! With one out in the eighth, rookie Robert Fick rocketed a grand slam off the rightfield roof — straight toward Comerica Park. The ball hit just to the foul-pole side of the light standard nearest the pole. For a second or two, everyone waited to see if it would bounce over the roof and become the final roof-clearing homer in Tiger Stadium. But it didn't quite make it.

No matter. Fick's NASA shot off Jeff Montgomery clinched the Tigers' 8-2 victory. The fans roared in jubilation worthy of the World Series as Fick slowly circled the bases. It was reminiscent of another eighth-inning, close-out homer: Kirk Gibson's second-deck blast off San Diego's Goose Gossage

Please see TIGERS, Page 6C

Damion Easley, left, Gabe Kapler, right center, and Karim Garcia, right, congratulate rookie Robert Fick after his grand slam drove in all of them in the eighth inning. It was the final hit in Tiger Stadium history.

Photos by KIRTHMON F. DOZIER (top) and JULIAN H. GONZALEZ (above)/Detroit Free Press

TIGERS
FINAL
LINEUP
AT THE CORNER

LF: LUIS POLONIA
2-FOR-3, HR

C: BRAD AUSMUS
1-FOR-3

1B: TONY CLARK
0-FOR-4

3B: DEAN PALMER
2-FOR-3

C: DAMION EASLEY
3-FOR-3

RF: KARIM GARCIA
1-FOR-3, HR

CF: GABE KAPLER
1-FOR-3

DH: ROBERT FICK
1-FOR-2, HR

SS: DEIVI CRUZ
0-FOR-4

P: BRIAN MOEHLER
6 IP, 2 ER

LHP: HAL
NEWHOUSER
1939-1953

LHP: MICKEY
LOLICH
1963-1975

RP: JOHN HILLER
1965-1970
1972-1980

MGR: SPARKY
ANDERSON
1979-1995

WORLD CHAMPIONSHIPS

1935:
Defeated the Cubs,
4 games to 2

1945:
Defeated the Cubs,
4 games to 3

1968:
Defeated the Cardinals,
4 games to 3

1984:
Defeated the Padres,
4 games to 1

APRIL 12, 2000 | COMMEMORATIVE SECTION

THE FIRST GAME

DETROIT FREE PRESS

MARINERS FIRST LINEUP
AT COMERICA PARK

LF: MARK McLEMORE
0-FOR-5

CF: MIKE CAMERON
0-FOR-4

SS: ALEX RODRIGUEZ
2-FOR-4

1B: JOHN OLERUD
3-FOR-5

DH: EDGAR MARTINEZ
0-FOR-5

RF: JAY BUHNER
3-FOR-5

2B: DAVID BELL
0-FOR-3

C: DAN WILSON
3-FOR-4

3B: CARLOS GUILLEN
1-FOR-3, 1 RBI

P: FREDDY GARCIA
6 IP, 5 ER

TIGERS FIRST LINEUP
AT COMERICA PARK

DH: LUIS POLONIA
1-FOR-4

2B: GREGG JEFFERIES
2-FOR-4, 2 RBIs

LF: BOBBY HIGGINSON
1-FOR-4, 2 RBIs

1B: TONY CLARK
1-FOR-4

C: BRAD AUSMUS
0-FOR-3

3B: DEAN PALMER
0-FOR-2

RF: KARIM GARCIA
0-FOR-4

CF: JUAN ENCARNACION
2-FOR-3

SS: DEIVI CRUZ
1-FOR-1

P: BRIAN MOEHLER
6 IP, 1 ER

	1	2	3		4	5	6		7	8	9		R	H	E
SEATTLE	0	0	0		1	1	0		0	0	0		2	12	2
DETROIT	2	2	0		0	0	1		0	0	x		5	8	3

Icebreaker

Tigers warm up quickly to new home with victory

BY JOHN LOWE
FREE PRESS SPORTS WRITER

All sorts of things happened in the first game at spacious Comerica Park that seldom or never would have happened at cozy Tiger Stadium.

Tigers catcher Brad Ausmus repeatedly called for pitches down the middle, inviting hitters to hit the ball toward the distant fences. Seattle never came close to hitting a home run, stranding runners galore in scoring position as Brian Moehler and his bullpen collected a 5-2 victory Tuesday before a capacity crowd of 39,168.

The Tigers parlayed walks and triples into two-run rallies in the first and second innings. They did something they did only five times the past two seasons at Tiger Stadium — win without a home run.

But one thing that never would have happened at Tiger Stadium had nothing to do with the change in ballparks. It had to do with 20 pounds that Tigers first baseman Tony Clark lost over the winter, making him faster on the bases and more agile on defense.

With none out in the sixth inning, with Moehler losing his stuff, and with the tying run on base, Clark dove to his right to rob Mark McLemore of the hit that could have turned the game around. Clark sprung up and tagged retreating Carlos Guillen for a rally-killing, unassisted dou-

Please see TIGERS, Page 9D

Photos by JULIAN H. GONZALEZ/Detroit Free Press

Todd Jones, who threw the last pitch at Tiger Stadium on Sept. 27, saved the first game Tuesday at Comerica Park.

Tigers first baseman Tony Clark tags Carlos Guillen to complete a double play in the sixth inning. Clark made a diving stop on a ball hit by Mark McLemore and beat Guillen to the bag. Both managers said it was the key play of the game.

FOR OPENERS

THE PITCH
At 1:18 p.m. Tuesday at Comerica Park, Tigers right-hander Brian Moehler delivered the first pitch — a fastball that Seattle's Mark McLemore took for strike one.

THE HIT
The first hit came in the first inning, from Seattle cleanup hitter John Olerud. He doubled down the rightfield line on Moehler's 19th pitch. The first Tigers hit came in the bottom of the inning, a leadoff triple by Luis Polonia on Freddy Garcia's third pitch.

THE NIGHT
Comerica Park's first night game starts at 7:05 tonight. The forecast: No TV. No rain. High of 46, low of 31. Tickets are available.

THE BOOK
Order our latest book, "Corner to Copa," and a poster of today's front page. See our advertisement on Page 6D or call 800-245-5082.

THE COVERAGE
Page 2D: Opening ceremonies, Steve Crowe's TV/radio column.
Page 3D: An essay on Copa.
Page 4D: Game 1 reviews: Food, service, rest rooms, etc.
Page 5D: Doron Levin's suite view.
Page 6D: Drew Sharp's column on injured Juan Gonzalez.
Page 7D: Players love the field.
Page 8D: They said it.
Page 9D: Box score, play-by-play.
Page 10D: A first-pitch poster.

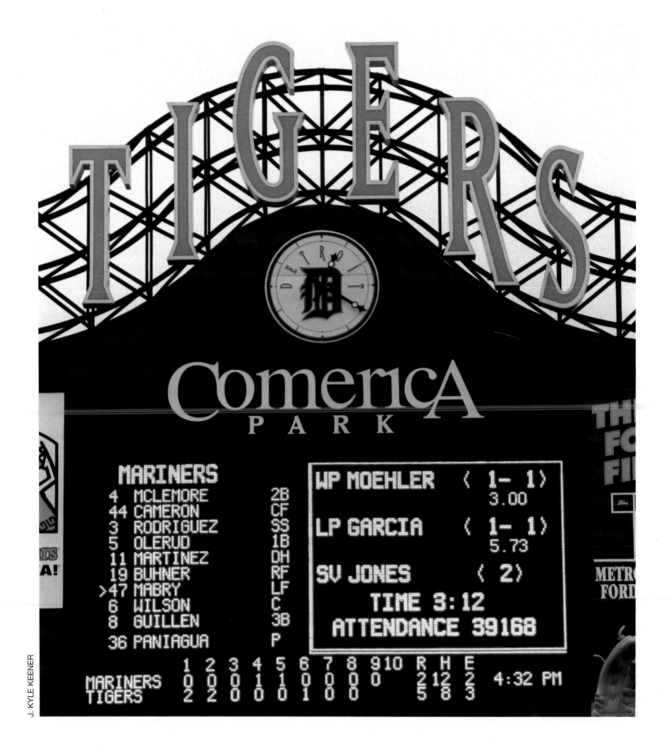

J. KYLE KEENER